THE OFFICIAL COOKBOOK

THE OFFICIAL COOKBOOK

RECIPES BY AUGUST CRAIG

TEXT BY JAMES ASMUS

INSIGHT
EDITIONS

SAN RAFAEL • LOS ANGELES • LONDON

CONTENTS

FOREWORD...8
INTRODUCTION.......................................10

BREAKFASTS...12
Not Megafruit Salad...............................14
Pancakes With Extra Syrup.................16
Pancake/Waffle Batter Mix...............17
Froopyland Waffles.................................19
Loaded Breakfast Hash Browns-.......20
Space Cruiser Sausage
and Gravy Biscuits.................................21
Morty's Face Breakfast Sandwich.......24
Mrs. Pancake's You Don't
Know Me Smoothie Bowl....................26
Mrs. Pancakes's Avocado Toast........29
Eye Holes..30
Jerry's PB&J French Toast...................35

APPS, SNACKS, SIDES.................37
Pickle Rick's Transformation Brine.......38
Multiverse Mushroom Canapés.........40
These Guys' Spinach
Artichoke Canapés................................41
Prosciutto Toast Canapés..................42

Detoxed Morty's Crudité....................43
Iceberg Wedge Salad.........................44
Immortality Snack Mix........................46
Riggity, Riggity Ranch.........................47
Mr. Beauregard's Memory Marmalade................48
Memory Making Cream Puffs............49
Lil' Bits Sandwiches..............................53
Lil' Bits Pies...54
Lil' Bits Fried Eggs..............................55
Lil' Bits Pizzas.......................................55
Bobish Potato Chips............................57

MAINS...59
Cronenberg Enchiladas........................61
Rick's Pork Scallopini..........................64
Sugar Chicken.......................................66
Frog Club Sandwich.............................69
Unity Burgers..70
Smith Family Pork Chops...................73
Hot Dogs on a Rick.............................75
Cauliflower Portal Mash.....................76
Ordinary Green Bean Casserole.......78
Just Cheesy Scalloped Potatoes.......79
Alternate Reality Pizza.......................80
Roy's Meat Loaf...................................83
Kale Salad..85
Roasted Acorn Squash Soup 86
Minestrone Soup..................................87
Roasted Tomato Pesto.......................88

Jerry's Singles Pot Pie 90

Jerry's Grilled Cheese 92

Jerry's Christmas Ham Glaze 93

Courageous Chili Dogs 94

DESSERTS 96

Kalaxian Crystals 98

Roy's Celebration Cake 100

Strawberries on a Cob 102

Dark Matter Brownies 105

Simple Rick Wafers 106

Mr. Nimbus's Beignets 108

True Level Lemon Bars 110

Strawberry Smiggles Bar 112

Spider Ice Cream 113

Supernova Tart 114

Jerry's Hungry for Apples Pie 117

DRINKS 119

Vat of Acid Margarita 120

Anti-Pickle Serum Shots 122

Multiverse Mojitos 124

Mr. Nimbus's Reserve Wine 125

Squanchy's Squanched Squanch Juice 127

Turbulent Juice 128

Beth's Homemade Lemonade 130

Detox Juice 131

Jerry's Sugar Water 132

SMITH-SANCHEZ FAMILY RECIPIES

HOME ECONOMICS—QUARTER PROJECT

by MORTY SMITH

Webster's Dictionary defines "MEAL" as "an act or the time of eating a portion of food to satisfy appetite."

And while we usually focus on the "food" part of our meals, this assignment made me start thinking about the "time" part.

The things we think of as "family recipes" are the ones that made an impression on us in the time we spent together. Either from taking the time to make something that requires a little extra love and special effort, or those dishes that become reliable traditions when the family is gathered together.

My family is a little unusual—so some of these recipes might be, too. (Um, not to break the formal project stuff, but—this might be the place to say that my Grandpa Rick in particular stormed off when I said I needed to get some family recipes. And when he gets like that, there's a pretty strong chance he's going to do something massively inappropriate to prove a point, or get his way, or just emotionally punish everyone involved in making him do something he doesn't like, so, if he slips something in here that isn't school appropriate, PLEASE know that it wasn't me, and don't detonate my grade without letting me fix it?)

But I'm glad this project asked me to take time to appreciate the different members and memories of my family. And I hope some of these might become a special "meal" for you and yours!

Meeseeks (and y'know, however many extra other Meeseeks you might recruit to help), I needed Morty for a space thing, but it'll probably take a week and he's freaking out about this stupid school project being a huge part of his grade (which I keep telling him is as important as being a "huge part" of a metaphorical element in a fart).

But Beth's been up my ass too, threatening to "restrict" my using Morty to "weekends," so let's just blow the doors off this ~~shit~~.

Go through my archives and gather or just *reverse-engineer* instructions on how to make anything and everything edible that comes up—to make the most epic, mind-blowing, and borderline weapons-grade cookbook in the history of the multiverse!!

Oh! And take some sick-~~ass~~ pictures to go with it! I'm not talkin' basic-~~bitch~~ brunch shots for your sad social media life—gimme some *reaaal* mouth-watering, give-your-stomach-a-boner pictorials! Maybe bust out the ol' SHRINK RAY (should be in the box of Anatomy Park merch) and get your camera *aaalllll* up in those juicy, dripping details. (Fair warning: If my dumb family sees you, they can't resist the urge to get shrunk and play "Ant-Person" or whatever sci-fi-for-toddlers shrinking story went around last.)

I don't even know what self-appointed, sad little Napoleon is ultimately gonna "grade" this thing. But let's see what you come up with.

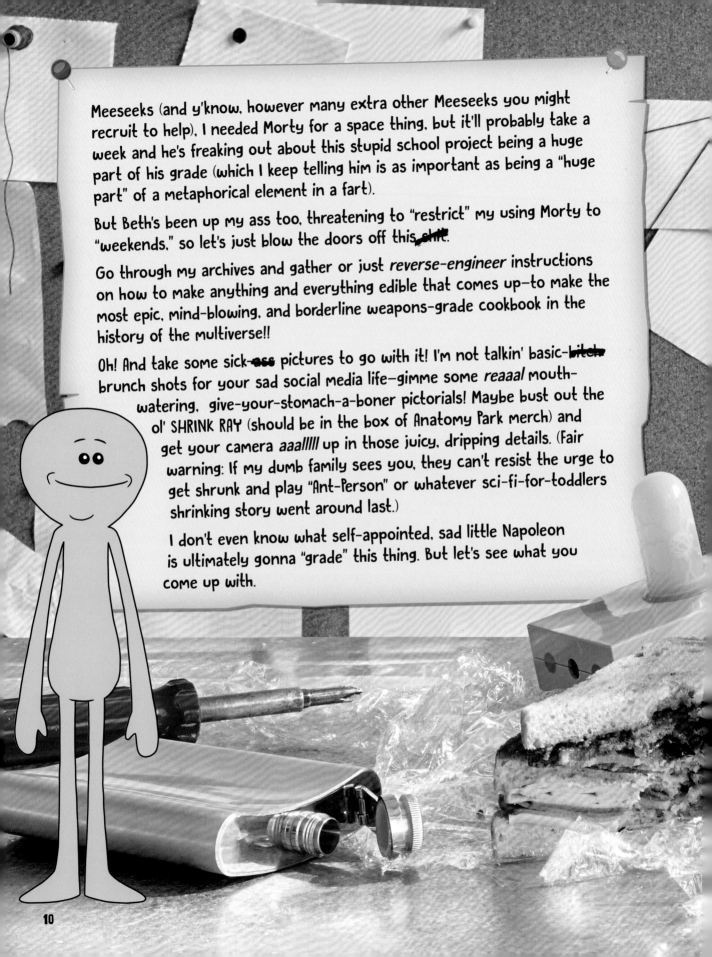

BREAKFASTS

BUTTERBOT_NARC-CAM_AUDIO-LOG_00152:

MORTY: Geez Mom, we—we have the same thing for breakfast ALL THE TIME! Can't you mix it up? I mean, I know the—the genre of "American breakfast food" is pretty LIMITED, but there's more than just PANCAKES—

BETH: Oh, excuse ME, your highness. I'm sorry you have a LOVING MOTHER getting up EXTRA EARLY to cook for you before she works to SUPPORT THE ENTIRE FAMILY.

MORTY: Ugh. Okay. I was just saying we could try—

BETH: If you're BRAINWASHED into wanting . . . STRAWBERRY SQWHATEVERS or . . . EYEHOLES from your INTERDIMENSIONAL TV commercials, ask your GRANDPA to bring something back from his trip besides MONSTERS and . . . SPACE HERPES!

MORTY: "Space herpes" would come from SPACE. We're talking about ALTERNATE-DIMENSIONAL—

GROWLING **CRASHING NOISES** **SHATTERING**

BETH: THERE! NO MORE PANCAKES! Have fun MAKING YOUR OWN WEIRD BREAKFAST.

NOT MEGAFRUIT SALAD

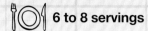 6 to 8 servings Prep: 25 minutes

Look, Morty—remember those MEGAFRUIT SEEDS? Well, since Grandpa isn't "legally" "allowed" to have "any" Megafruit in this region of the galaxy, I'm definitely "not using code" here when I ask you to make this this totally normal "NOT MegaFruit Salad." (But you'll know you made it right if—after you try some - you can lift the neighbor's house.)

1 pineapple

3 green kiwis

1 white dragon fruit

2 yellow peaches

One cup (6 ounces) of blueberries

1½ cups (10 ounces) of sliced strawberries

Juice from ½ a lemon

1. Cut pineapple in half lengthwise and then cut out core from both sides.

2. Carefully score inside of pineapple in a grid pattern.

3. Scoop flesh from inside pineapple halves, leaving enough structure for use as a bowl later.

4. Peel and dice kiwis into chunks.

5. Peel and dice dragon fruit into chunks.

6. Cut peaches in half to remove each pit, then cut into slices.

7. Rinse and dry blueberries, discarding any stems.

8. Hull and slice strawberries into quarters.

9. Squeeze or pour lemon juice over fruit.

10. Gently combine so as not to damage fruit slices as they are placed back into each pineapple half for serving.

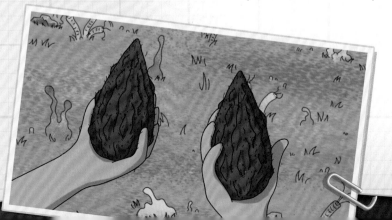

And now—
Devour the fruits and feel the power of a god coursing through your veins!! You'll be impervious! You're unstoppable!!

PANCAKES WITH EXTRA SYRUP

 10 to 12 pancakes

Prep: 25 minutes
Cook: 35 minutes

As far as family recipes go, this one might be one of our most cherished. Pancake breakfasts are as close as you can get to a Sanchez family tradition—and this is the way my mom always made her pancakes on special occasions. With extra love.

I don't get to make it as often as I'd like. But I'm happy to share it here and hope it winds up spreading a little more of the specialness my mother always tried to add to the world.

FROM THE DESK OF JERRY SMITH!

Well what does it take to get some of that "extra love" thrown my way?! I ask for Special Pancakes all the time!

FOR THE MAPLE CHIPS

 About 2 cups maple chips

 Prep: 20 minutes (mostly time spent waiting for the sugar to cool)
Cook: 15 minutes

1 cup maple syrup
1 tablespoon powdered sugar

1. Heat maple syrup in a small saucepan and bring to a gentle simmer, then carefully bring the syrup up to 300°F (hard-crack stage).

2. Pour hot syrup onto a parchment-lined, rimmed baking sheet, and spread thin with a spatula.

3. Allow molten syrup to cool until hard at room temperature.

4. Use the back of a spoon to break up hard sheet of dried syrup.

5. Place maple chips into a container, dusting with powdered sugar to coat. These can be stored at room temperature for up to 2 weeks.

PANCAKE/WAFFLE MIX

 About 8 cups pancake mix   **Prep: 10 minutes**

6 cups all-purpose flour
1½ cups powdered buttermilk
¼ cup sugar
3 tablespoons baking powder
1 tablespoon baking soda
3 teaspoons kosher salt

1   Mix ingredients into a bowl. Can be used immediately, or saved for the next time pancakes or waffles are cooked.

PANCAKE BATTER

 4 to 6 people
(about 9 to 12 pancakes depending on size)   **Prep: 5 minutes**
Cook: About 5 minutes per pancake
(45 minutes total cook time)

1½ cups premade pancake mix
1 cup water (add as needed for consistency)
1 egg and 1 egg yolk
2 tablespoons butter, melted
1 teaspoon vanilla extract
Maple chips

1   Combine ingredients in a large bowl and whisk together. Batter should be slightly lumpy, so be sure not to overmix!

2   Heat skillet on medium and grease with a small pat of butter.

3   Using a ¼ measuring cup, scoop batter onto a hot skillet.

4   Once batter is placed, drop a few maple chips onto pancake and gently press down.

5   Flip pancakes as batter bubbles to surface and begins to pop.

6   Keep pancakes warm in the oven at 200°F until ready to serve.

FROOPYLAND WAFFLES

 6 to 8 waffles

Prep: 10 minutes
Cook: 20 minutes

Beth, here's the recipe for FROOPYLAND WAFFLES.
But I only made these because you were
TERRIFYINGLY OBSESSED with your private
FANTASY LAND as a kid. I know adulthood is
depressing, but so is choosing "nostalgia"
as your escapism when I could send you
LITERALLY ANYWHERE IN THE MULTIVERSE.

1½ cups premade pancake/
waffle mix
(same as previous pancakes)

1 cup water (add as needed
for consistency)

1 egg and 1 egg yolk

2 tablespoons butter, melted

1 teaspoon vanilla extract

One 4-pack food coloring
(any colors can be used)

1   Combine ingredients (except food coloring) in a large bowl and whisk together. Batter should be slightly lumpy, so be sure not to overmix!

2   Separate waffle batter equally into four containers.

3   Add 5 to 10 drops of food coloring to each container and mix thoroughly.

4   Place approximately 1 tablespoon of each color mix onto the waffle iron, drizzling each color in different places/patterns.

5   Cook waffles following waffle iron cooking instructions.

Mom, can you give me a few more recipes for this thing? There's not enough breakfast. Maybe, like, potatoes or something?

How much TIME does your STEPFORD SCHOOL think we HAVE in a day?! I gave you PLENTY, and at this point I REFUSE to believe you're really learning anything by making your PARENTS compile a bunch of COOKING INSTRUCTIONS.

Here's two choices, Morty—put in note that says "MY MOM SAID JUST BUY FROZEN HASH BROWNS LIKE A NORMAL PERSON WHO WAS UP TOO LATE DRINKING AWAY THE REGRET OF A TEACHING DEGREE" or open the internet for something besides PORN and REVENGE-DOXXING YOUR SISTER and print a damn recipe yourself.

anyrecipe.com

Home > Recipes > Breakfasts

Loaded Breakfast Hash Browns

SAVE   PRINT   SHARE

Servings: 4 to 6   **Prep:** 15 mins   **Cook:** 35 mins

Ingredients

- ☐ 5 pieces bacon, crumbled
- ☐ One 20-ounce bag shredded hash browns
- ☐ 2 tablespoons neutral cooking oil
- ☐ ¼ cup shredded cheddar cheese
- ☐ 2 stalks green onion
- ☐ 2 tablespoons sour cream

Directions

1. Preheat the oven to 250°F.

2. Cook bacon using the desired method until crispy, then crumble and set aside.

3. Heat oil in a large oven-safe skillet over medium heat. Once hot, place hash browns in an even layer and press into the pan.

4. Cook until a golden crust forms, then start flipping hash browns in sections.

5. Once all hash browns are cooked through with a crust on both sides, top with shredded cheese and bacon.

6. Place into a preheated oven for approximately 5 minutes, until cheese is melted.

7. Thinly slice green onions.

8. Top hash browns with sour cream and green onions, then serve hot.

SPACE CRUISER SAUSAGE AND GRAVY BISCUITS

 6 to 8 servings

 Prep: 40 minutes
Cook: 45 minutes

Okay—just to be clear, the family cookbook assignment mentioned "extra credit" if we make a NEW recipe that's something personal to us, right? Because that's what this one is. I made it.

I mean, it's actually my mom's recipe for the biscuits. (Or wherever she got it, I guess? She's not really like a "food experiment" person.)

And my uncle Steve taught me how to make the sausage gravy. (Or, at least, he IMPLANTED a fake, parasitic memory of teaching me how. (Because it turned out he was a psychic alien parasite. (Which was a huge bummer, when he was the only person in my family who actually made me feel good about myself.)))

But look! I put that stuff together with eggs and some sausages to make a fun—and neat?—little ship! It's like a spaceship. Specifically, like my grandpa's.

Anyway, I thought that would be fun. Because that's a way cooking can be like life, maybe?

We take all the different weird stuff our families dump into our brains and pump down our throats—and we try to stack it all up, somehow, into something that can carry us forward?

FOR SAUSAGE GRAVY:

Two 8-ounce packages breakfast sausage links

¼ cup flour

3 cups whole milk

½ teaspoon ground white pepper

15 turns black pepper from a grinder

⅛ teaspoon ground nutmeg

1½ teaspoons salt

2 teaspoons maple syrup, stirred in at the end

FOR BISCUITS:

4 cups flour, with ½ cup reserved to coat surface and hands

4 tablespoons powdered buttermilk

2½ teaspoons baking powder

2 teaspoons kosher salt

1½ teaspoons sugar

¼ teaspoon baking soda

1 cup (2 sticks) butter, cut into small pieces and chilled

1 cup cold water

2 tablespoons butter, melted for brushing

FOR ASSEMBLY:

1 sunny-side-up egg per biscuit

CONTINUED ON NEXT PAGE . . .

TO MAKE SAUSAGE GRAVY:

1 Cook 1 package of sausage links. Set aside and keep warm.

2 Drain fat from the pan and cook a second package of sausage links. This group of links will be broken into small pieces.

3 Once sausage is browned, stir in flour and cook for about 2 to 3 minutes until the raw-flour smell is gone.

4 Drizzle in milk slowly while whisking to prevent lumps.

5 Once gravy is smooth, add white pepper, black pepper, nutmeg, salt, and maple syrup.

6 Set aside and keep warm.

TO MAKE BISCUITS:

7 Preheat the oven to 400°F.

8 Place flour, powdered buttermilk, baking bowder, kosher salt, sugar, and baking soda in a large bowl and mix thoroughly.

9 Add chilled butter pieces. Use a pastry cutter to mix until remaining butter pieces are pea-size.

10 Slowly pour in cold water and mix with a fork until a shaggy ball of dough forms.

11 Place dough on a clean, flat surface and shape into a 1-inch-thick square.

12 Using a knife, cut dough into 4 equal pieces and stack.

13 Roll stack into a 1-inch-thick rectangle.

14 Using a round biscuit cutter, cut 12 biscuits out of dough and place on a parchment-lined baking sheet, then freeze for 10 to 15 minutes.

15 Brush tops of biscuits with butter and bake for 20 to 25 minutes until golden brown on top.

NOTE: Biscuits can be frozen uncovered until solid, then transferred to a bag or container and kept for about 1 month. Do not thaw before baking.

FOR ASSEMBLY:

16 Pour ¼ cup sausage gravy onto a plate to create an "asteroid belt."

17 Top 1 biscuit with fried egg to create the dome canopy of Rick's car.

18 Put ½ sausage link on either side of biscuit to make the engines of the car.

19 Place completed biscuit car onto gravy asteroid belt and enjoy.

MORTY'S FACE BREAKFAST SANDWICH

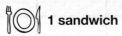 1 sandwich   Prep: 10 minutes
Cook: 10 minutes

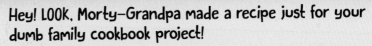

Hey! LOOK, Morty—Grandpa made a recipe just for your dumb family cookbook project!

It's your dumb face. As a sandwich.

I'm actually pretty pleased with this one, because every time you whine about school, or grades, or girls who don't like you, I WANT TO LITERALLY CHEW YOUR FACE OFF.

And now I can!

So can you—whoever the hell is supposed to be reading this—EAT MORTY'S DUMB FACE! MMM... that's some tasty, tasty EFFIGY right there!

2 pieces bacon

2 eggs

1 plain bagel

1 tablespoon butter

Ring mold approximately the size of a bagel

Salt

Pepper

2 slices American cheese

1 Cook bacon using desired method.

2 Carefully separate yolks from egg whites, keeping yolks aside and intact.

3 Toast bagel and set aside.

4 Heat butter in a skillet on medium heat and place a ring mold in the skillet.

5 Pour egg whites into the ring mold, then gently press the mold down to prevent any egg leaking.

6 Using a rubber spatula, gently place 2 egg yolks on whites to make the Morty eyes.

7 Sprinkle with salt and pepper to taste.

8 Cover the skillet with a lid and allow egg to cook.

9 Slice bagel in half, placing 1 slice of cheese on each side.

10 Place egg face on bottom 2 slices of bagel.

11 Arrange 1 slice of bacon under yolk eyes to create a smile.

12 Set 2 top pieces of bagel to make Morty's hair.

Mom said I can't take the car for Tricia's party unless I help you with your stupid recipe book so here—I ripped out a couple pages from one of the magazines you stash under your bed. Byeeee!

COQUETTE
MAGAZINE

EVERYONE'S DYING TO KNOW THREE THINGS AFTER LAST SEASON'S CLIFF-HANGER SEASON FINALE OF THE SEXY SMASH HIT SERIES

1 **WHO** did she end up in bed with on that Costa Rican yacht?! Armand DeGuapo, or Bud Chucklet??

2 Can society ever truly achieve **JUSTICE** when progress is only pursued through the lens of lessening systemic harm to the targeted and historically disadvantaged—but refuses to reckon with the generations of wealth and opportunity **STOLEN** by the advantaged, and their more deeply entrenched resistance against efforts to **TAKE BACK** any wealth that stems from historic injustice?

3 **HOW DOES MRS. PANCAKES KEEP SUCH A SEXALICIOUS BIKINI BOD?!?**

Well on those first two, we'll have to wait until the next season premiere and an inevitable blood-drenched class reckoning, respectively. But **COQUETTE** managed to pry a couple hints on the LAST (most important?) one from **MRS. PANCAKES** herself!

Here's the **TWO** go-to breakfasts this star-**STUNNING** actress allows herself during swimsuit season! (Which, for someone whose career hinges entirely on elderly male entertainment executives finding her bangable, is forever!) Yaaas, Queen! Dish!

MRS. PANCAKE'S
YOU DON'T KNOW ME SMOOTHIE BOWL

Serves: 2 bowls   **Prep: 25 minutes**

½ **cup apple juice**

1 cup frozen fruit mix (strawberries, pineapple, mango)

Two 3½-ounce packs frozen acai berries

½ **cup frozen blueberries**

1 tablespoon chia seeds

1 cup choice granola

1 cup fresh raspberries

4 tablespoons unsweetened coconut flakes

1 Blend together ¼ cup apple juice with frozen fruit mix, then set aside in the refrigerator to (like your bestie always tells you) "CHILL!"

2 Blend remaining ¼ cup apple juice with acai and frozen blueberries!

3 Stir chia seeds into acai blueberry mix and set aside in the refrigerator, grrl!

4 Allow chia seeds to bloom as both mixtures chill for 15 minutes!

5 Working with 2 bowls, pour half of acai mixture into each bowl!

6 Add even portions of frozen fruit mixture to each serving! You GOT this, bossanista!

7 Using a spoon, gently swirl mixtures together to create a fun cosmic pattern!

8 Garnish with granola, raspberries, or coconut flakes, then enjoy.

COQUETTE
LIFE HACK

You can experiment with substituting other fruits for fun, variety, and taste while still getting the natural vitamins and antioxidants that help keep your skin looking young enough to meet the crushingly limited societal definition of beauty!

MRS. PANCAKES'S AVOCADO TOAST

Serves: 4   **Prep: 15 min**   **Cook: 20 min**

FOR CROSTINI:
24 slices baguette (approximately half a baguette)

2 tablespoons olive oil

½ tablespoon kosher salt

FOR SEASONING:
1 teaspoon sesame seeds

1 teaspoon poppy seeds

1 teaspoon dried onion, minced

1 teaspoon dried garlic, minced

½ teaspoon kosher salt

FOR AVOCADO FILLING:
2 ripe avocados

½ lime, juiced

Reserve 1 teaspoon prepared seasoning as topping

1   Preheat the oven to bake at 350°F.

2   Cut baguette into thin diagonal slices.

3   Arrange slices on a baking sheet, brushing each slice with olive oil.

4   Sprinkle baguette slices with salt.

5   Bake for about 20 minutes.

6   Set salt and toast aside. Mix remaining seasoning ingredients in a dry pan and toast for 3 to 5 minutes until seeds begin to crack.

7   Pour into a small bowl and add salt.

8   Cut avocados in half, then scoop flesh into a bowl. Be careful to keep avocado rind intact.

9   Squeeze lime over avocado before adding seasoning, then mix until combined and add black pepper to taste.

10 Carefully spoon avocado filling back into avocado rinds, then gently press 6 crostini into each half of avocado and serve.

EXCLUSIVE!

THE ESSENTIAL "MRS. PANCAKES"

Favorite line from the show so far?

"You don't know me!"

Three things the character and I BOTH can't live without?

Water, oxygen, and the sun, probably?

If I didn't get into acting, I'd be . . . ?

Committing murders for national attention.

EYE HOLES

 15 to 20 Eye Holes

Prep: 25 minutes
Cook: 20 minutes

Here you go, Jerry—I reverse-engineered and chemically approximated a way to make your own things that TASTE just like Eye Holes—WITHOUT attracting that psychotic little violence goblin, EYEHOLE MAN.

So, that means, keep your dirty dumbass hands off MY authentic Eye Holes. AND if you can't keep your stupid mouth shut and wind up drawing him here just by SAYING "Eye Holes" too much, you're on your own this time, and I hope he beats you to death slowly enough that you have time to think about what a sad, pointless little life you lead.

Merry Christmas. Don't say I never gave you anything.

FOR DOUGH:

2 cups cashews

1 cup old-fashioned oats (gluten-free if necessary)

½ cup dates, pitted

½ cup shredded coconut, unsweetened

2 bananas

1 cup freeze-dried strawberries

1 tablespoon honey

FOR FILLING:

1 cup vanilla yogurt (nondairy if necessary)

1 teaspoon wheatgrass powder

1   Preheat oven to 350°F.

2   In a food processor, pulse together cashews, oats, dates, and coconut for 1 to 2 minutes until well blended. Transfer mixture into a bowl and set aside.

3   Next, blend bananas, dried strawberries, and honey in the food processor until a paste has formed, about 30 seconds. Once blended, add date mixture and pulse together for 1 minute.

4   Scoop out 2 tablespoons of dough at a time and form into an oblong ball with a divot in the center. Pinch edges together slightly to "close the eye," but make sure not to seal shut. Bake for 15 to 20 minutes on a baking sheet lined with parchment paper or a silicone mat.

5   While Eye Holes are baking, whisk together yogurt and wheatgrass powder in a small bowl. Once mixed, transfer to a small squeeze bottle or pastry bag with a small tip. After Eye Holes are removed from the oven and cooled slightly, fill divot in center with yogurt.

Beth!

I think I just invented the next great American Menu Item!

I know you wanted some time alone, but I really think this could be huge. Between your brains and my legally protected idea (I sealed an envelope and mailed it to myself—so it's got that post office date that's as good as a copyright!—this could be our ticket to Millionaires-burg!!

I know you'll probably think this is some sad attempt to get you back (or at least to return a message!), but would a sad loser have spent the last 3 weeks only making French toast until he found a NEW way to make it that feels like being back in the safety and happiness of childhood?

At least make it, and tell me what you think? Or I can come over in the morning and make it for you!

Yours, (not that you WANT me anymore!) (HA! That's just a joke.)

Jerry

JERRY'S PB&J FRENCH TOAST

 8 to 10 French toast pockets

 Prep: 35 minutes
Cook: 35 minutes

INGREDIENTS! :-)

For the custard:

⅔ cup half-and-half

4 eggs

1 tablespoon powdered sugar

1 teaspoon vanilla extract

½ teaspoon cinnamon

Pinch salt

For assembly:

Loaf sandwich bread (white bread works best)

One 16-ounce jar peanut butter (or nut spread of choice), ½ tablespoon per sandwich

One 18-ounce jar strawberry jam (or jam of choice), ½ tablespoon per sandwich

½ tablespoon butter for pan

¼ cup powdered sugar for topping

HOW TO MAKE IT :-o

1 In a medium bowl, whisk together all ingredients for custard for 1 to 2 minutes until thoroughly combined. Transfer to a shallow dish and set aside. This will be the dipping station.

2 To assemble a French toast pocket:

3 Cut crusts off 2 pieces of bread, making them as square as possible. Press a circular divot into center of each slice of bread. With bread flat, deposit peanut butter and strawberry jam onto 1 piece of bread and lay over the top.

4 Seal PB&J pocket by pinching edges together all around with tines of a fork.

5 Warm butter in a skillet.

6 Dip sandwich pocket into custard and coat on all sides. Be careful not to soak bread in custard too long, or bread will fall apart.

7 Fry in skillet 1 to 3 minutes per side until golden brown. Can be kept warm in a low oven on a cookie sheet while you repeat with the rest of bread and filling.

8 Dust with powdered sugar and serve warm.

APPS, SNACKS & SIDES

Okay, now we're talking! APPETIZERS, SNACKS, and SIDE DISHES are Jerry Smith's middle names!

Life's so full of different flavors, of possibilities! Why NOT treat yourself to little tastes of so many new things?

It's the same reason I've come to appreciate all the different twists and turns in life that let me experience so many different job opportunities! I mean, did I originally WANT to keep a steady career that would reliably provide for my family as I gained more respect and rewards from my work over the years? Sure! But then I never would have dabbled in app developing or writing fan fiction!

And if I only ever stuck with my "main dish," Beth, I never would have opened my horizons to incredible "saucy side dishes" like Mr. Nimbus, the King of the Ocean, and Sleepy Gary—or "gooey finger foods" like that alien huntress I dated! ← *OH MY GOD DAD, PLEASE CUT THAT OUT AND REPRINT THIS!!*

So, of course, I love ACTUAL appetizers and great sides, too!

But it is a lot of work to make a BUNCH of stuff. So, I don't really do it. Ooh! But since recipes are simple enough, I could make a Meeseeks do it! (Make some appetizers. Not like, "do it" do it.)

↑ *THIS TOO!!*

PICKLE RICK'S TRANSFORMATION BRINE

 1 jar of 6 pickles   Prep: 15 minutes
Cook: 10 minutes

You ready to make some gorgeous PICKLES, Morty? I'm talking some reaaaaaal beauties. Perfect, sour, wart-covered representations of humanity's ability to TRANSFORM NATURE into something BETTER! But so simple, even a remedial mind like yours can do it.

But for real—you BETTER DO THIS ONE. The public demands more "Pickle Rick"—but I need some DECOYS. So . . . y'know . . . try to make 'em reaaaal SULTRY PICKLES, just like Grandpa.

1 sealable jar large enough to hold pickling items (tall, wide-mouth 24-ounce mason jar)

6 Persian cucumbers, rough ends cut off

FOR BRINE:

¾ cup cold water

½ cup white vinegar

¼ cup rice vinegar

½ tablespoon kosher salt

¾ teaspoon sugar

½ tablespoon black peppercorns

½ teaspoon coriander seed

¼ teaspoon crushed red pepper

½ teaspoon fennel seed

1 bay leaf

3 cloves garlic, lightly crushed

2 to 3 sprigs of fresh dill

1 Combine water, both white and rice vinegars, salt, and sugar into a measuring cup, then set aside.

2 In a warm pan, toast peppercorns, coriander, red pepper flakes, fennel seed, and bay leaf until fragrant. Stir often to prevent burning.

3 Combine toasted spices and brine mixture into a medium pot and bring to a simmer.

4 Place crushed garlic, dill, and cucumbers into the pickling jar and make sure everything fits nicely.

5 Carefully pour hot brine into the jar until it covers cucumbers.

6 Seal the jar and allow it to cool to room temperature before refrigerating. Pickles are ready to eat the next day; however, the longer they sit, the more flavorful they become. Can be stored in the fridge for about 2 months.

MULTIVERSE MUSHROOM CANAPÉS

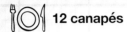 12 canapés

 Prep: 15 minutes
Cook: 25 minutes

AUDIO RECORDING TRANSCRIPT—RICK'S LAB_3756A$$

RICK: Morty, you need to MEMORIZE this one in case I'm ever taken hostage . . . You're gonna go, and you're gonna make these canapes EXACTLY as I tell you—got it?

MORTY: Ooh—are they, like . . . secretly POISON or make guys EXPLODE or something?

RICK: It's FOOD, Morty! People don't—*buuurp*—they don't KILL THE HOSTAGE if someone just hooked 'em up with some tasty canapes! Seriously, Morty—ALL ALIEN PHYSIOLOGY is DIFFERENT. I can't give you ONE RECIPE to KILL EVERY SENTIENT BEING IN THE MULTIVERSE! . . . Well, I COULD. But you'd need *reaaal* weird stuff for that one. This mostly needs MUSHROOMS. And mushrooms grow wherever it's DARK, COLD, and ROTTING—which basically describes ALL OF EXISTENCE.

12 crimini mushrooms, STEMS REMOVED!!

1 shallot, finely minced

¼ cup panko bread crumbs

½ cup (about 4 ounces) shredded Gruyère cheese

1 egg

2 tablespoons parsley, chopped

2 tablespoons unsalted butter or olive oil for brushing

Zest of ½ lemon

1. Preheat the oven to 350°F.

2. Remove each mushroom cap from stem.

3. Dice mushroom stems and shallot, then combine in a bowl with bread crumbs, cheese, and egg. Mix until combined.

4. CAREFULLY stuff mixture back into mushroom caps.

5. Brush with 2 tablespoons of unsalted butter or olive oil.

6. Bake at 350°F for approximately 20 minutes.

7. Can be made up to a day in advance and stored in the refrigerator until ready to bake.

8. Extra leftover filling is perfect for scrambled eggs.

Then stop to appreciate how if you weren't so chickens**t, and trusted the intergalactic nuclear military-industrial complex, you wouldn't have to waste brain cells on CAVEMAN BULL***T like "PREHEATING"!

I stress the point because I've seen you get sloppy with NITROGLYCERIN, MORTY.

That's more time than it would take me to BUILD A GIGATON REACTOR OVER—but, hey, it's your fleeting life. Spruce up both with a squeeze of lemon zest.

So, you should make me some. When I'm hung over.

THESE GUYS' SPINACH ARTICHOKE CANAPÉS

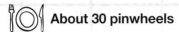 About 30 pinwheels

 Prep: 1 hour, 30 minutes
Cook: 15 minutes

2 sheets puff pastry
(17.3 ounces)

2½ ounces fresh spinach,
stemmed

4 cloves of garlic, minced

One 8.5-ounce can of artichoke
hearts, minced

1 tablespoon olive oil

1 tablespoon salted butter

1 teaspoon salt

Black pepper to taste

One 8-ounce block cream
cheese, softened

½ cup grated Parmesan cheese

1 tablespoon chives, minced

1 tablespoon minced parsley

½ tablespoon lemon juice

1   Preheat the oven to 400°F.

2   Defrost 2 sheets of dough from 1 package of puff pastry according
to instructions.

3   Sauté spinach, artichoke hearts, and garlic in 1 tablespoon olive
oil and 1 tablespoon butter.

4   Thoroughly combine softened cream cheese, Parmesan, chives,
parsley, and lemon juice with cooked spinach-and-artichoke mix.
Allow to cool completely before spreading on pastry dough.

5   Unfold puff pastry and roll into an approximately 9-by-14-inch
rectangle. Spread about half of the filling evenly on sheet of pastry
dough, then repeat for second sheet. After spreading filling onto
each sheet, refrigerate each for approximately 10 minutes.

6   Roll both pastry sheets into tight logs, starting from the bottom.

7   After rolling, place into freezer to firm for at least 15 to 20 minutes.

8   Take logs out of the freezer and, using a sharp knife, cut thin slices
down length of log. (After cutting, they can be frozen for up to 2
months.)

9   Bake at 400°F for 10 minutes, then at 350°F for
15 to 20 minutes until golden brown and firm.

10   Allow to cool for 10 minutes before serving.

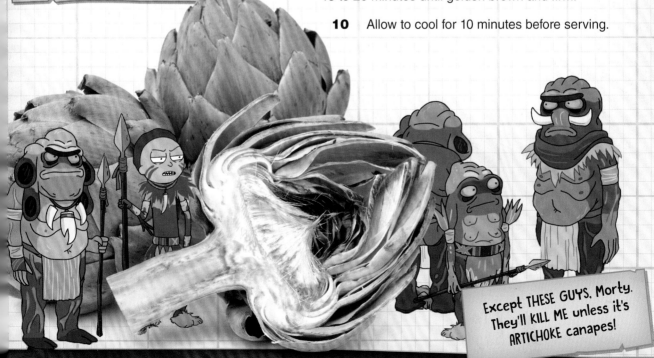

Except THESE GUYS, Morty.
They'll KILL ME unless it's
ARTICHOKE canapes!

41

PROSCIUTTO TOAST CANAPÉS

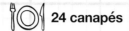 24 canapés Prep: 20 minutes
Cook: 5 minutes

Ingredients

6 slices quality sourdough bread with crust removed, sliced into quarters

1 tablespoon olive oil

½ cup fig jam

1 teaspoon fresh ground black pepper

½ teaspoon rice vinegar

About 4 ounces soft Brie cheese

One 3-ounce package prosciutto

1 or 2 thyme sprigs for garnish

1   Preheat the oven to 350°F.

2   Remove crust from bread, then cut slices into even quarters.

3   On a baking sheet, toast bread slices for 5 minutes.

4   While bread is toasting, combine fig jam, black pepper, and rice vinegar in a small bowl, then set aside.

5   Cut Brie into thin, small slices sized to fit bread.

6   Slice prosciutto into thin ribbons.

7   Assemble canapés by spreading ½ teaspoon of jam mixture onto toast, followed by a slice of Brie, then prosciutto.

8   Garnish with a sprinkle of thyme leaves on top.

DETOXED MORTY'S CRUDITÉ

 4 to 5 servings Prep: 10 minutes

Hi Morty!

It's me, Morty. But I'M the you who just got back from a real swell spa weekend and is living his best, freshly detoxified best life!

While I've got a clear head (and heart and pores, ha ha!), I just figured I'd leave a few helpful reminders to my future, eventually stressed self, y'know? And seeing the family recipe book made me think, maybe things don't always need to be COMPLICATED and TIME CONSUMING? Maybe sometimes we should just CUT UP SOME HEALTHY, NATURAL FOODS and call it a job well done! So, here's your permission to do yourself that favor today!

No need to thank me—you ARE me! Just consider regularly whipping up one of these bad boys (or should I say GOOD boys?!), and we'll STAY our best selves! (No matter WHAT wacky hijinks we get up to!)

Namaste,
"Detoxed" Morty

1 large English cucumber

1 red bell pepper

1 yellow bell pepper

2 medium carrots

1   Peel and deseed cucumber before slicing it into sticks.

2   Peel carrots and cut into long slices.

3   Core bell peppers and slice into sticks.

4   Serve on a platter with Riggity, Riggity Ranch (page 47).

*Note: We remember "Toxic" Morty, right? Well I prefer it when our FOOD is green—not US! Ha ha LOL

ICEBERG WEDGE SALAD

 10 to 12 salad skewers   **Prep:** 20 minutes
Cook: 25 minutes

JERRY. WHY did I just have to sign for a package that turned out to be this recipe for Iceberg Wedge Salad from the Titanic: Experience the Romance company and a notarized letter from their LAWYERS?

Because it LOOKS like you signed something saying you hold them IN NO WAY responsible for hiring and retaining the insane woman who held you hostage, tried to assault you, and would have KILLED YOUR WIFE—IN EXCHANGE FOR AN APPETIZER RECIPE.

Do us both a favor and DO NOT <u>ATTEMPT</u> to explain yourself until you are <u>ABSOLUTELY CERTAIN</u> the words you're planning to say won't make this WORSE.—Beth

10 to 12 wooden skewers
5 to 6 bacon slices, crumbled
½ cup toasted walnuts
1 head iceberg lettuce
1 or 2 large vine tomatoes
1 large red onion

FOR DRESSING:
½ cup mayonnaise
1 cup sour cream
2 tablespoons lemon juice
1 tablespoon Worcestershire sauce
2 cloves garlic, minced
4 ounces blue cheese, crumbled
½ teaspoon salt
Ground black pepper to taste

1 Preheat the oven to 400°F.

2 Cook bacon using the desired method until crispy, then crumble and set aside.

3 Toast walnuts in a dry pan for 5 minutes (if unsalted, add a pinch), then set aside.

4 Use a fork to combine mayonnaise, sour cream, lemon juice, worcestershire sauce, garlic, blue cheese, and salt in a measuring cup. (Substitute blender or food processor for a smoother dressing.) Finish dressing with ground black pepper to taste and give one final stir.

5 Slice vegetables into wedges (larger chunks than would normally be in a salad), then set aside.

6 Skewer vegetables in an alternating pattern, leaving a small section of empty skewer at the base to keep fingers clean while holding.

7 Arrange on a platter and drizzle with desired amount of dressing. Remaining dressing can be placed in a serving container and available on the side.

8 Top dressed salad skewers with toasted walnuts and crumbled bacon.

IMMORTALITY SNACK MIX

 About 16 servings

Prep: 5 minutes
Cook: 25 minutes

Well, I've never had too much luck with cooking. (I bet you're saying "Or anything else!" But you're no America's Funnyman, Jimmy Fallon, so spare me the jokes!) But as the patriarch of this family, I scrapped together some fun recipes of my own!

One tasty little treat I like to make for myself is my own IMMORTALITY SNACK MIX! I modeled it off of the really yummy free (!) snacks they had at a bar on the Resort Planet, where—get this!—you can never die! (I mean, some people DID die. But only after Rick messed things up.) But after a bunch of weekdays alone in the house experimenting with my own recipe (thanks, unemployment!), I perfected a recipe that makes me FEEL immortal all over again!

---

9 cups square corn cereal

3 cups mini pretzels

2 cups cashews

1 cup almonds

1 cup roasted sesame sticks

½ cup (1 stick) of butter, melted

⅓ cup Worcestershire sauce

1 tablespoon kosher salt

½ tablespoon garlic powder

1 teaspoon onion powder

1 teaspoon ground black pepper

1 teaspoon green matcha powder

---

1   Preheat the oven to 275°F.

2   In a large bowl, combine corn cereal, pretzels, cashews, almonds, and sesame sticks. Mix until items are evenly mixed.

3   Melt butter, then whisk together with Worcestershire sauce, salt, garlic powder, onion powder, black pepper, and green matcha powder. Pour mixture over snack mix and toss until coated.

4   Line two rimmed baking sheets with parchment paper, add butter-coated mix, then bake for 20 to 25 minutes until mixture is dry.

5   MOST IMPORTANT: Remember—25 minutes is a long time, but DON'T FORGET you're waiting for that and, say, fall asleep in the closet after taking a "me time" break browsing adult sites. Because the mix will eventually burn and set off all the smoke alarms, and the fire department blocked our number. (Even though THEY were the ones who barged in and woke ME up! I wasn't "tricking them" into seeing ANYTHING!)

RIGGITY, RIGGITY RANCH

 About 3 cups of dressing

 Prep: 5 minutes
Cook: 10 minutes

```
AUDIO RECORDING TRANSCRIPT—RICK'S LAB_34TA$$

This is IT. Th-this is the BREAKTHROUGH—the, the SINGLE GREATEST
DISCOVERY of ALL my life's work!

A SICK-*SS RANCH DRESSING!

Seriously. I know there are… a BILLION ones in the world already.
But—but those are all CREAM from a CORPSE'S BALLS compared to THIS!
And, and I'm NOT just s-so HYPED because I'm [BELCHES] [CONTINUED
BELCHING] drunk.

[INAUDIBLE] . . . Okay, isss a little that I'm drunk . . . [SNORING]

[18 MINUTES ELAPSE]

Huh—?! [MUMBLES] Oh, S**T, yeah! Copume . . . COMPUTER! Finalize that
last essperiment. Project file: [BELCHES] RIGGITY, RIGGITY RANCH, son!
```

¾ cup aquafaba (water in which chickpeas have been cooked)

½ teaspoon cream of tartar

2 tablespoon Dijon mustard

1 teaspoon garlic powder

2 teaspoons onion powder

½ teaspoon ground black pepper, or to taste

½ teaspoon salt

½ cup neutral oil such as avocado or grapeseed

¾ olive oil

1 cup loosely packed herbs and leaves, such as parsley, chives, thyme, basil, oregano, and rosemary

1 In a blender, add aquafaba and cream of tartar. Blend on low to combine, then continue to blend on high for 2 minutes.

2 Add Dijon mustard, garlic powder, onion powder, black pepper, and salt, then blend on high for another 30 seconds to combine.

3 Mix neutral oil and olive oil together.

4 With the blender running on low, pour in a steady stream of oils until all are incorporated. Use the blender spout or pour hole. If no spout is available, add oil in small amounts and blend between additions.

5 Finely chop herbs, adding to the blender a handful at a time. Blend for 30 seconds to combine.

6 Decant dressing to an airtight container and refrigerate until needed. Molecular analysis suggests this can be stored for 1 week.

They say that *smell* is the sense most closely linked to memory. But I believe a well-cooked meal, or even a simple snack prepared with care and familiarity, can transport us all instantly back to fine times fondly recalled.

After my years of diligent care and service as the Smith family's devoted butler, to find my loyalty—nay, my entire identity—called into question is admittedly heartbreaking.

But I present these few of the countless recipes I have prepared in my decade of time with you all in hopes that reexperiencing their delights may provoke precisely such evocative experiences to serve as a flashback to simpler times and a reminder of our many, many years together.

Your faithful butler, family confidant, and definitely not an alien parasite falsifying memories,

MR. BEAUREGARD

Hey, Mom—It's a bummer that Mr. Beauregard turned out to be an alien parasite or whatever—but these recipes are LEGIT! KEEP MAKING 'EM!!
—Morty

MR. BEAUREGARD'S MEMORY MARMALADE

 about 6 4-ounce jars

 Prep: 15 minutes
Cook: 25-30 minutes

2½ cups fruit, 3 to 4 navel oranges

½ lemon, juiced

4¼ cups sugar

¾ cup water

One 3-ounce package pectin

1 stick cinnamon

1 pod star anise

1 Using a vegetable peeler, carefully shave off only colored parts of orange and lemon peels, making sure to leave white pith behind. Cut shaved peels into very thin ribbons and then set aside in a bowl.

2 With a paring knife, cut both ends off of citrus. Stand fruit on a flat end, then, using a downward knife cut, remove remaining pith.

3 To remove fruit segments, cut along inside of each membrane at an angle toward core. Remove slice of fruit, roughly chop, then place in a bowl with rind and repeat for entire orange. Mix in lemon juice, cinnamon, and star anise. Measure 2⅓ cups of fruit mixture into a bowl. If necessary, supplement with water for an exact measurement. Combine sugar, then let stand for 10 minutes, stirring occasionally.

4 Mix water and pectin in a small saucepan. Bring to a boil, stirring constantly for 1 minute, add fruit mixture, then stir for about 3 minutes until sugar is dissolved.

5 Once sugar is dissolved, pour the mixture into clean jars and seal. Let stand at room temperature for 24 hours or overnight. Mixture can be stored in refrigerator for up to 3 weeks. Marmalade can be frozen for up to 12 months, but make sure to leave room in the container for marmalade to expand as it freezes.

MEMORY MAKING CREAM PUFFS

 About 24 cream puffs

 Prep: 1 hour
Cook: 35 minutes

FOR THE PATE A CHOUX PASTE:

½ cup whole milk

¼ cup unsalted butter, cut into tablespoon-size chunks

½ tablespoon sugar

¼ teaspoon salt

½ cup all-purpose flour

2 eggs, room temperature

FOR FILLING:

⅛-ounce block cream cheese, softened

2 tablespoon parsley, chopped

2 tablespoon chives, chopped

1 teaspoon salt

Black pepper to taste

1½ tablespoon lemon juice

½ English cucumber, peeled and finely minced

1 Line 2 cookie sheets with a silicone mat or parchment paper. Preheat the oven to 400°F.

2 In a large saucepan over medium-high heat, combine milk, butter, sugar, and salt.

3 Bring to a boil and add flour all at once. Stir vigorously with a wooden spoon until mixture is smooth and is not sticking to the spoon or pot. If mixture looks rough or butter leaks out, keep stirring until it comes together. Once mixture is smooth and formed into dough, remove it from the heat and transfer to a bowl.

4 Allow mixture to cool for 5 minutes and then begin adding eggs 1 at a time. Beat mixture smooth again after adding each egg to ensure it is completely incorporated.

5 Fill a large pastry bag fitted to a plain ½-inch tip with pate a choux. Pipe balls approximately 1 inch in diameter onto the cookie sheets, spaced about 2 inches apart. Dip a finger in water, then gently smooth out tip left after lifting the bag.

6 Bake for 10 minutes, then reduce the oven temperature to 350°F. Bake for another 20 to 25 minutes, or until golden brown and firm to the touch.

7 With a sharp skewer or the tip of a paring knife, poke a small hole in bottom of each puff, then place puff back on the cookie sheet upside down (or on side) to allow steam to escape while cooling. Store in an airtight container until ready to fill. Makes about 24 puffs.

8 Combine filling ingredients into a bowl and mix together with a fork until fully incorporated.

9 Transfer filling into a pastry bag fitted with a small pastry tip (size 8 round or .17-inch diameter opening) and squeeze about ½ teaspoon of filling into each puff from the bottom. Be careful not to overfill puff, or the ratio of filling to dough will be incorrect.

10 Serve and enjoy.

Meeseeks—I need a full spread of this stuff for a peace summit with the Squirrels. I know they usually eat nuts and s**t, but they're omnivores. Basically, rats with better P.R. So, let's blow their tiny minds and bury the hatchet so I don't have to nuke another dimensional reality.

LIL' BITS

RECIPE GUIDE

Welcome to your new career as a chef for Lil' BITS family restaurants!

Remember. Our customers' mouths are tiny and small. That's why they come on down to Lil' Bits. So we make food that looks like regular food, but really tiny.

Every dish should live up to the Lil' Bits promise: "You put it in your mouth and you eat it. Nothing gets stuck in your lips. It's just tiny, and tiny, and fits right in."

So, make some tiny s**t, you stupid a**h**e! Ha ha—just kidding.

LIL' BITS SANDWICHES

 18 mini sandwiches

 Prep: 25 minutes
Cook: 15 minutes

One 6-pack frozen breadsticks

3 slices Swiss cheese (or preferred variety)

3 slices deli turkey (or preferred meat)

2 to 3 baby greens per sandwich

3 to 4 cherry tomatoes

¼ red onion

1 pickle

FOR EACH SUB:

1 baked breadstick

½ teaspoon mayonnaise

½ teaspoon mustard

½ piece Swiss cheese

½ slice deli turkey

½ leaf lettuce

1 cherry tomato, sliced into rounds

2 thin onion slices

2 to 4 pickle rounds (use pickles you make from the apps section)

1 Cook breadsticks according to package instructions ahead of time. Allow to cool before making sandwiches.

2 Slice breadstick lengthwise and spread mayo and mustard on either side.

3 Arrange cheese triangles along the bottom half of breadstick.

4 Cut turkey into 2 to 3 pieces and place on sandwich, being sure to cover cheese.

5 Roll lettuce leaf and slice into ribbons, then arrange atop turkey.

6 Arrange tomato, onion, and pickle onto sandwich and top with other half of breadstick. Slice into 3 mini sandwiches.

7 Repeat with remaining breadsticks.

LIL' BITS PIES

 12 mini pies

 Prep: 1 hour, 25 minutes
Cook: 20 minutes

FOR PIE DOUGH:

1¼ cups all-purpose flour

1 teaspoon powdered sugar

½ teaspoon salt

¼ cup (½ stick) unsalted butter, very cold

2 tablespoons solid vegetable shortening, very cold

About ⅓ cup ice water

FOR FILLING:

½ cup sugar

2 tablespoons cornstarch

¼ teaspoon ground allspice

10 ounces blueberries, frozen

3 tablespoons lemon juice

2 tablespoons milk for bruising on top

2 tablespoons sugar for topping

1. Preheat oven to 425°F.

2. Using a pastry cutter, combine flour, powdered sugar, salt, butter, and shortening into a bowl.

3. Once pieces of butter and shortening are about the size of peas, begin pouring in cold water a small amount at a time (you might not use all of it), and mix by hand until mixture comes together into a loose dough.

4. Turn dough out onto a floured work surface and roll out to ⅛-inch thick. Then cut out 12 circles, each 2½ inches in diameter, using a cookie cutter or small glass. These will be the base of pies. Gently press circles of dough into a mini muffin pan and refrigerate for 20 minutes.

5. To make pie tops, cut 12 circles at 1½ inches in diameter, then place on a parchment-lined baking sheet and refrigerate for 20 minutes.

6. For filling, combine sugar, cornstarch, and allspice in a bowl with frozen blueberries and mix to coat. Add lemon juice and set aside for 5 minutes.

7. Transfer filling to a small saucepan and heat on medium low until mixture begins to simmer. Warm for about 10 minutes, stirring occasionally, to prevent burning. Mixture will be done when thick and glossy. Set aside and allow to cool.

8. Once cool, dollop 1 teaspoon of filling into base of each pie, then place pie tops over the filling. Crimp along edges using a toothpick, Poke 3 small venting holes into pie tops. Brush each pie with milk and sprinkle a small amount of sugar on each. Bake for 15 to 20 minutes until golden brown.

LIL' BITS FRIED EGGS

 4 to 5 mini fried eggs

 Prep: 10–24 hours (eggs freeze overnight)
Cook: 5 minutes

1 large egg

½ tablespoon butter

Salt and pepper to taste

1   Freeze egg overnight or until completely solid. When egg is frozen, crack and remove shell. Running warm water over egg may help shell separation.

2   With shell removed, use a sharp knife to carefully slice egg into rounds.

3   Melt butter in a small saucepan on medium-low heat and place slices of egg in the pan. Cover with a lid and cook eggs until whites are set but yolk is slightly runny (about 3 to 5 minutes), then transfer to a plate and season to taste with salt and pepper.

LIL' BITS PIZZAS

 24 mini pizzas

 Prep: 30 minutes
Cook: 10 minutes

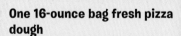

One 16-ounce bag fresh pizza dough

One 8-ounce bag pepperoni

Pizza sauce from Alternate Reality Pizza

One 6-ounce bag shredded mozzarella

1   Preheat oven to 425°F.

2   Working on a well-floured surface, make a 1½-inch ball of pizza dough, then press flat and spread into a circle. Place 1 teaspoon pizza sauce into middle of dough, then spread evenly over surface. Sprinkle ½ tablespoon shredded cheese over top of pizza.

3   Using a large straw or pastry tip, cut out approximately 7 mini circles of pepperoni from 1 normal slice, then arrange mini pepperonis onto pizza. Next, transfer completed pizza to a parchment-lined cookie sheet and set aside. Repeat with remaining ingredients.

4   Once pizzas are assembled, bake in the oven for 5 to 10 minutes. Be sure to keep an eye on these, as they can burn quickly. Serve and enjoy.

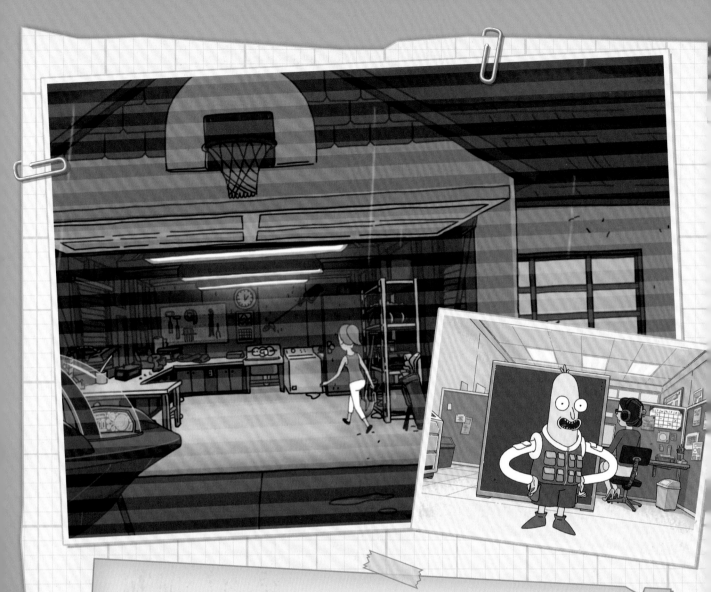

SECURITY LOG: 9:18PM
NOT-RICK IDENTIFIED: SUMMER
THREAT ASSESSMENT: WON'T STAY OUT OF MY SHI-

AUDIO RECORDING TRANSCRIPT—RICK'S LAB_RU486

HEY, SO, COMPUTER? YOU CAN, LIKE, MAKE STUFF, RIGHT?
MAKE MORE OF THESE ALIEN CHIPS. I LIKE THESE CHIPS.

*BEGINNING CRUMB AND GREASE ANALYSIS . . . CREATING
APPROXIMATION WITH AVAILABLE MATERIALS . . . .*

BOBISH POTATO CHIPS

 6 servings

Prep: 2 hours, 30 minutes
Cook: 5 minutes

FOR SALT AND PEPPER SEASONING:

2 teaspoons fresh ground black pepper

1 teaspoon kosher salt

FOR CHIVE AND CHEDDAR SEASONING:

2 teaspoons chives, dried

1 teaspoon cheddar cheese powder

¼ teaspoon kosher salt

FOR CAJUN/BBQ SEASONING:

1 teaspoon ancho chili powder

½ teaspoon ground cumin

½ teaspoon onion powder

½ teaspoon garlic powder

¼ teaspoon mustard powder

¼ teaspoon smoked paprika

1   To slice each potato, hold it vertically and carefully press against a mandoline on its thinnest setting.

2   Place potato slices into a large bowl and cover with cold water, allowing to soak for 2 hours. After 1 hour, change water, adding more salt for the second hour-long soak.

3   In a large Dutch oven, heat oil to 350° to 375°F.

4   After potatoes have been soaked, drain and transfer to a baking sheet lined with a kitchen towel, then pat as dry as you can. When dry, fry several at a time. Using a spider strainer or slotted spoon, gently flip each slice. Once very lightly blonde (about 1 minute total cooking), take chips out and drain on a paper towel-lined baking sheet. Repeat until all slices are cooked.

5   Combine ingredients of desired seasoning. Sprinkle with seasoning very shortly after pulling from the fryer to be sure it sticks to chips.

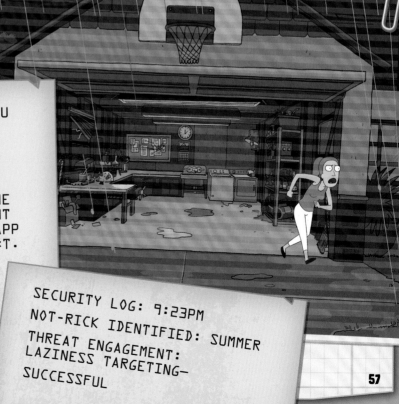

UH . . . OKAY . . . SO, ARE YOU GONNA MAKE THOSE, OR . . . ?

ACTIVATING: MESSAGE FROM RICK: S05 8B . . .

"SCREW YOU, SUMMER. THIS IS THE MOST ADVANCED DIGITAL ASSISTANT IN THE UNIVERSE, NOT A PHONE APP FOR FEEDING LAZY PIECES OF S**T. MAKE WHATEVER TRASH YOU ASKED FOR YOURSELF."

BOOO . . . JERK. LIKE ANYONE WOULD DO ALL THAT FOR CHIPS.

SECURITY LOG: 9:23PM
NOT-RICK IDENTIFIED: SUMMER
THREAT ENGAGEMENT:
LAZINESS TARGETING—
SUCCESSFUL

MAINS

A great meal needs a great main course.

Something that's comforting, nourishing, but still has some fun or surprise in it.

Which, now that I say it, sounds a lot like what it takes to be a great mother!

I mean, not to flatter myself _too_ much, but the comparison is pretty true. The main dish provides so much of what you need out of a meal, and does so much _heavy lifting_ that all the other little side dishes are free to go off in all their own weird little directions, even if they never wind up being something "satisfying" or "healthy" or "employable."

I mean, does that sometimes put _too much_ pressure on the main dish? OF COURSE. How is any _one_ recipe supposed to be able to wrangle three or four different appetizers and sides constantly bickering, or disappearing, or bringing unimaginable chaos and aliens and existential NIGHTMARES to the table _every—single—DAY_?!

Maybe it should be comforting to know there's _another_ main dish out there, made from the exact same recipe?

CRONENBERG ENCHILADAS

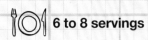 6 to 8 servings

 Prep: 1 hour, 25 minutes
Cook: 1 hour, 45 minutes

I love enchiladas. I–I know that's probably not established anywhere. But I'm establishing it NOW. Rick is a *biiiiig* enchila-daddy!

But ever since that ONE TIME I accidentally mutated everyone in Morty's original dimension into horribly mutated flesh-glob CRONENBERG MONSTERS, he absolutely can't handle seeing GOOEY, SLOPPY, RED ENCHILADAS without bursting into tears!

But guess what, Grandpa still loooooooves his enchiladas! And if I don't get to have 'em WHENEVER I WANT, I might just make THIS world all CRONENBERGED! So SUCK UP those TEARS, Morty! Because now I want enchiladas! And seriously, the salt—the salt from your tears would throw off the whole flavor matrix.

FOR MOLE SAUCE:

1 tablespoon oil for pan

½ yellow onion, diced

3 cloves garlic, minced

1 jalapeño, seeded and minced

2 tablespoons raisins

1 tablespoon chili powder

½ teaspoon ground cinnamon

½ teaspoon ground coriander

2 tablespoons bread crumbs

1¼ cups vegetable broth

1 dried bay leaf

2 tablespoons unsweetened cocoa powder

1 tablespoon smooth almond butter

½ tablespoon ketchup

½ teaspoon salt

FOR CHICKEN:

1 pound boneless skinless chicken thighs

¼ cup mole sauce to coat

FOR ENCHILADA SAUCE:

1 tablespoon vegetable oil in saucepan

½ yellow onion

2 cloves garlic, minced

One 4-ounce can mild green chilies, diced

1 bay leaf

1 teaspoon oregano

1½ teaspoon ground cumin

One 28-ounce can tomato puree or sauce

1 cup veggie broth

FOR BEANS:

1 can black beans

1 dried bay leaf

1 teaspoon kosher salt

FOR ENCHILADAS:

8 ounces shredded cheddar cheese

20 count bag 6- to 8-inch flour tortillas

CONTINUED ON NEXT PAGE . . .

TO MAKE MOLE SAUCE:

1   Heat a large saucepan with oil. Sauté onions until translucent.

2   Add garlic, jalapeño, and raisins, then sauté until vegetables are soft.

3   Stir in chili powder, cinnamon, coriander, and bread crumbs. Cook 3 to 5 minutes until mixture begins to stick to the bottom of the pan.

4   Slowly add in broth, stirring to scrape up fond from the bottom of the pan.

5   Simmer for 10 minutes, then remove from heat. Blend with an immersion blender until smooth. (A regular blender can be used instead, but the mixture must be cooled before use. Once it is smooth, add it back to pan.)

6   Add in bay leaves, cocoa powder, almond butter, ketchup, and salt. Stir to combine, and simmer for another 15 minutes. Set aside.

TO MAKE CHICKEN:

7   Preheat the oven to 425°F.

8   Place chicken thighs on a rimmed baking sheet.

9   Coat each thigh on both sides with mole sauce.

10 Bake for 20 to 25 minutes until the internal temperature reaches 165°F.

11 Remove from the oven and let rest. When cooled, use 2 forks to shred chicken, then set aside.

TO MAKE BEANS:

12 Pour beans into a small pot, then add bay leaf and salt.

13 Warm through, and then set aside.

TO MAKE ENCHILADA SAUCE:

14 Heat a sauce pot with oil, then sauté onions until translucent.

15 Stir in garlic and diced green chilies, bay leaf, oregano, and cumin, then saute for another 5 minutes.

16 Add tomato sauce and veggie broth. Bring to a gentle simmer for 10 minutes, and set aside.

TO ASSEMBLE ENCHILADAS:

17 Preheat the oven to 375°F.

18 Combine 6 ounces of shredded cheese, shredded chicken, and beans (bay leaf removed) for enchilada filling.

19 Pour ¼ cup of enchilada sauce in the bottom of a 9-by-13-inch glass baking pan, then spread evenly.

20 Carefully dip 1 tortilla into pot of enchilada sauce to coat, then put 2 tablespoons of filling into middle of tortilla.

21 Carefully roll tortilla and place seam side down into the baking pan. Repeat until the pan is filled.

22 Pour remaining enchilada sauce evenly over top of assembled enchiladas.

23 Cover with foil, and then bake for 20 minutes.

24 Once enchiladas are bubbling, uncover and top with remaining 2 ounces of shredded cheese and bake for another 10 minutes until cheese layer is crisp.

25 Serve with remaining mole sauce on the side.

RICK'S PORK SCALLOPINI

 5 to 6 servings Prep: 1 hour, 45 minutes
Cook: 1 hour

Hi Beth, honey—While I'm still living in a moment of CLARITY after a shockingly effective DETOX treatment, I really want to make you that SCALLOPINI I offered.

Knowing "regular Rick," I'm sure it won't be long until we let regret, ego, and hedonism turn us right back into a Rick so distracted by his own crap that he forgets all about it.

Sadly, I think somewhere in repeated use of the Mindblower "toxic me" already wiped out any memory of how to MAKE it the way you used to love. But how does this recipe sound?

One 16-ounce package of pasta

6 quarts water for pasta

5 pork chops, cut thin

Salt and pepper to season pork

1 cup flour

1 tablespoon butter

2 tablespoons capers

2 cloves garlic, minced

¼ cup white wine

1 lemon, juiced

1 tablespoon caper juice

1 teaspoon fresh thyme, minced

1 teaspoon chopped parsley and more for garnish

1. Set a large pot to boil with about 6 quarts of water. Once it is boiling, place pasta into water and stir to make sure pasta does not stick together. Boil pasta for 8 to 10 minutes until al dente. Drain and keep warm on the side; optionally, add small pat of butter or dash of olive oil to cooked pasta and stir to coat.

2. Season each side of pork chops with salt and pepper.

3. Dredge each side in flour, making sure to press pork down into flour to coat evenly.

4. Place butter in pan and heat until foaming. When butter foams, fry pork chops in batches, about 5 minutes on each side, until golden brown (internal temp 145°F). Set aside and keep warm in oven at a low temperature.

5. Once all pork chops are cooked, fry capers and garlic, then sauté for 2 minutes. Deglaze with wine and lemon juice, then add ¼ cup pasta water to emulsify the sauce. Add in thyme and parsley and simmer sauce for 1 to 2 minutes to allow flavors to infuse.

6. Place pork chop over a bed of pasta. Top with lemon caper sauce and chopped parsley.

Post-detox selfie.
Don't you want to
hang onto being this
content and centered
version of yourself—for
your family—as long as we
can?

They've had enough of
our TOXIC side, I'm sure.

SUGAR CHICKEN

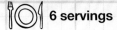 6 servings

 Prep: 1 hour
Cook: 35 minutes

Once our children got a little more adventurous in trying new foods, they soon fell in love with going out for Sugar Chicken at various Chinese restaurants on a Friday night. But soon, there were more than a few stretches of time where their father would wind up out of a job, and we had to find ways to cut costs and get by on just a horse surgeon's salary.

They were sad to lose the tradition, but I promised the kids I'd learn how to make it at home, researching recipes and trying different approaches until we found our favorites!

But after a few weeks of whining and pouting that a MEAL I COOKED AFTER A LONG AND BLOODY DAY UP TO MY ELBOWS IN EQUINE INTESTINES "didn't taste right", we all realized it was easier to force Jerry to take a job as a dishwasher in one of the kitchens at least long enough to learn how to make it the NEXT time he gets fired. WIN-WIN! (And the answer was six days. He lost the dishwashing job in SIX DAYS.) So, hopefully, this recipe lets YOU skip past the months of criticism from armchair food critics who SHOULD be saying "THANKS, MOM! WE LOVE YOU!"

1 cup orange juice

1 orange, zested

2 tablespoons rice vinegar

3 tablespoons soy sauce

½ teaspoon sesame oil

1 teaspoon aji mirin

6 tablespoons brown sugar

2 cloves garlic, grated

½ teaspoon fresh ginger, grated

½ teaspoon red pepper flakes

½ tablespoon cornstarch for sauce

¼ cup water

6 cups oil for frying

4 cups white rice

1 cup cornstarch for dredging

½ cup flour

2 eggs

2 pounds boneless skinless chicken thighs, cut into 1-inch cubes

4 stalks green onion, sliced thin

1. Combine orange juice, orange zest, rice vinegar, soy sauce, sesame oil, and aji mirin in a saucepan, then bring to a simmer.

2. Add brown sugar, garlic, ginger, and pepper flakes. Continue to simmer for about 5 minutes.

3. Combine ½ tablespoon cornstarch and water to make a slurry. Slowly whisk slurry into the sauce over low heat to thicken. Once thick and glossy, set aside.

4. Heat oil to 350°F in a large Dutch oven.

5. Cook rice according to package instructions (rice cooker recommended).

6. Combine 1 cup cornstarch and ½ cup flour into a shallow dish, then set aside.

7. Crack 2 eggs into a shallow dish and whisk together. Set aside.

8. Dredge chicken pieces in batches first into flour-cornstarch mixture, then into egg, then back into mixture.

9. Once fully coated, fry chicken in batches for about 5 to 10 minutes until golden brown and cooked through.

10. When all chicken is cooked, place into a large bowl and drizzle sauce over chicken. Toss to combine and then serve warm over rice. Garnish with green onion.

Hello Rick,

If you are reading this, I'm dead.

But as I sit here still alive, I have been reflecting fondly on everything you've given me. Friendship. Inspiration. A place of incredible peace, beauty, and contemplation in which I can drop my pants to my ankles and lay out even the most devastating of turds with zero self-consciousness and merciful air circulation.

And with all you've shared, I wanted to share something in return. It's a small gesture, but consider it a memento of my appreciation and the many bonds we now share. Not the least of which is my use of your previously private toilet.

When you analyzed my intestinal detritus and tracked me down, you asked, "Was it worth it?"

Now that you and I are connected, I can easily answer, "yes." But when, at the time, I was merely considering the club sandwich I had consumed earlier from a frog-run restaurant near my work . . . ?

I'd probably say yes then too. It's a very good sandwich.

So I went to the trouble of compiling its recipe as best I could. I hope it brings you even a sliver of the joy and serenity your private pooping place has brought me.

Always keeping the seat warm for you,

Tony

FROG CLUB SANDWICH

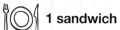 1 sandwich

 Prep: 15 minutes
Cook: 25 minutes

3 pieces sourdough sandwich bread, toasted to preference

½ tablespoon mayonnaise

1 slice Swiss cheese

2 to 3 slices deli turkey

2 to 3 slices Black Forest ham

1 tablespoon pesto (see Roasted Tomato Pesto, page 88)

½ cup baby spinach, stemmed

2 round slices tomato

2 to 4 pieces bacon, depending on size

2 pimento olives

1   Cook bacon until crisp using your desired method.

2   Spread mayonnaise on 2 slices of bread, then place Swiss cheese on one slice. This will be the bottom of the sandwich.

3   Add alternating layers of sliced ham and turkey. Top with an additional piece of bread, mayonnaise side down.

4   Spread top of bread with half of pesto, and set the rest aside.

5   Stack spinach onto top of sandwich to begin creating top layer of sandwich. Layer tomato and bacon, then top with last piece of bread and add remaining pesto. Garnish with olives and serve.

6   Makes a sandwich for one—but that doesn't mean you're alone.

UNITY BURGERS

 6 to 8 burgers   Prep: 45 minutes
Cook: 25 minutes

As an expansive, contagious, hive-mind consciousness entity, I have absorbed a nigh-infinite amount of knowledge and experience from my hosts across countless civilizations.

The mind of Unity holds experiences and discoveries from millions of lifetimes—wisdom from countless choices and outcomes, the expertise of the greatest luminaries in all fields of study, memories of those who witnessed the rarest phenomena in scientific or metaphysical truth!

So, with no pretense of humility, but full confidence in the truth of this statement, I can assure you—this is how to make some absolutely sick-ass burgers!

5 slices bacon, crumbled

8 ounces block Gruyère cheese, shredded

1 tablespoon butter, softened

2 pounds ground beef

2 tablespoons Worcestershire sauce

Black pepper to taste

1 teaspoon salt

6 burger buns

1. Cook bacon with preferred method and then crumble, combining with shredded cheese and butter. Scoop out ½-tablespoon balls and set aside on a plate in the refrigerator to chill until ready to form patties.

2. In a large bowl, combine ground beef, Worcestershire sauce, salt, and pepper, then mix thoroughly. Using a kitchen scale, measure 4-ounce balls of meat and set on a parchment-lined baking sheet to store.

3. Working with your hands (or the hands of others that you control through your networked but overriding consciousness), form each ball into a round patty with a small divot in the center. Place a ball of bacon-and-cheese mixture into center of burger, then carefully wrap meat from one ball around filling and enclose it, making sure to seal any gaps. Repeat with remaining burgers and filling.

4. Once all burgers are filled and shaped, place in the refrigerator to chill for at least 15 minutes or up to 4 hours.

5 Preheat grill or cast-iron skillet on medium-high heat. Once grill is heated, place burgers onto the cooking surface and sear for 3 to 5 minutes until char/crust has formed. Flip burgers and sear other side for 3 to 5 minutes as well. Use a cooking thermometer to ensure desired temperature:

Medium-rare at an internal temperature of 130° to 135° F (55° to 57° C)

Medium at an internal temperature of 135° to 150° F (57 to 65° C)

Medium-well at an internal temperature of 150° to 165° F (65° to 74° C)

Well-done at an internal temperature of 165° F (74° C) or greater.

6 Remove burgers from the cooking surface and transfer to a plate.

7 Finish with favorite burger sauces and toppings if desired.

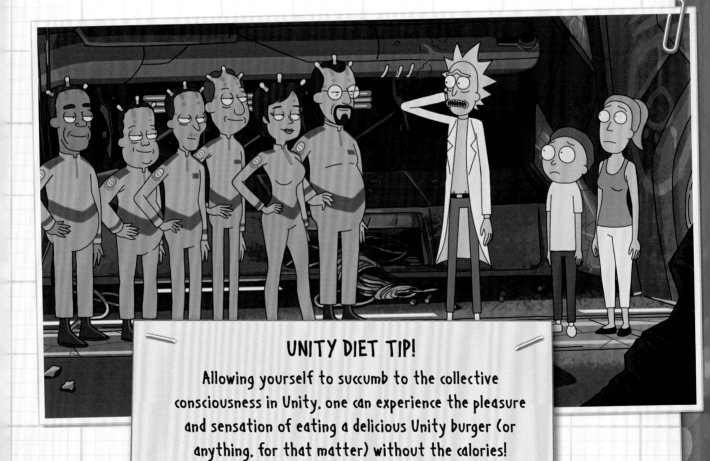

UNITY DIET TIP!
Allowing yourself to succumb to the collective consciousness in Unity, one can experience the pleasure and sensation of eating a delicious Unity burger (or anything, for that matter) without the calories!

This is another Smith-Sanchez household favorite recipe, and one that I tweaked and evolved over the first few years of cooking for my own family. When I was an independent woman studying medicine and then working my way through horse-surgeon residency, I'd never even imagine taking the time to cook full and well-prepared meals for myself. But suddenly, once I had children of my own (and the adult-child I married) to take care of, I wanted to make the time to build up some dishes that made everyone happy, healthy, and at home. After countless little experiments (just like Dad, I guess!), this version proved to be the winner. Enjoy!

I CALL BULLS**T! Seriously, Mom, when you lay it on this thick, I totally know you're overcompensating for something.

Thanks to, y'know, SEARCH ENGINES, it took TWO SECONDS to find this recipe word-for-word in a 2008 blog post called "EASY RECIPES FOR RELUCTANT MOTHERS"!

As disturbing as that part is, let's just skip to me saying this is good for one "Mom Doesn't Get to Say ANYTHING If/When Summer Gets Busted for Plagarizing Her Homework."

SPECIAL COUPON

Mom Doesn't Get to Say ANYTHING If/When Summer Gets Busted for Plagarizing Her Homework.

SMITH FAMILY PORK CHOPS

 6 servings   Prep: 30 minutes
Cook: 25-30 minutes

½ cup Dijon mustard

1 teaspoon Worcestershire sauce

1 tablespoon honey

2 teaspoons apple cider vinegar

Pepper to taste

1 clove garlic, finely minced

6 pork chops, tenderized

1 Preheat oven to 400°F.

2 Whisk Dijon mustard, Worcestershire, honey, vinegar, garlic, and pepper in a measuring cup and set aside.

3 Cut a long sheet of parchment paper and bring the ends together, folding in half. This will create an area to tenderize pork chops.

4 Open folded parchment and place 1 pork chop onto it, then fold the parchment back over so that pork chop is covered top and bottom.

5 Using a meat tenderizer or heavy flat skillet, flatten pork chop evenly, but not so thin as to tear holes in the paper or pork chop. Set aside onto a rimmed baking sheet and repeat with remaining pork chops

6 Once pork chops have been tenderized, deposit 1 tablespoon mustard sauce onto each pork chop, being careful not to touch pork chops with the measuring spoon. Next, using a silicone brush, spread sauce evenly over each pork chop, making sure to coat all sides. Once all pork chops are coated, place into the oven until internal temperature reaches 145°F, or about 25 minutes.

7 If any mustard sauce is left over, heat in a small saucepan over medium low and simmer for 3 to 5 minutes. This can be served to top pork chops.

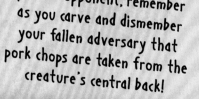

HAMURABI TIP!
If you choose to honorably battle and slay your own porcine opponent, remember as you carve and dismember your fallen adversary that pork chops are taken from the creature's central back!

HOT DOG ON A RICK
Employment Application

I AM A: MORTY ☐ IRREPARABLY, SEVERELY DAMAGED RICK ☐

HOME DIMENSION: _____

PREVIOUS WORK EXPERIENCE (Besides being your Rick's Morty): _____
_____

KNOWN ALLERGIES, CONDITIONS, MUTATIONS, IMPLANTS, OUTLIER HOME WORLD PHYSIOLOGY, INTERDIMENSIONAL DISEASES, PARASITES, LASTING PHYSICAL OR PSYCHOLOGICAL TRAUMAS:

_____
_____
_____
_____
_____
_____
_____
_____
_____
_____
_____

I SWEAR TO YOU, MORTY, IF YOU PUSH FOR ANOTHER "CITADEL" ADVENTURE (A PLACE THAT OF COURSE STILL EXISTS AT THE TIME I'M WRITING THIS), I WILL ABANDON YOU IN THE BLEAKEST BOWELS OF THEIR SOLIPSISTIC RETAIL DISTRICT.

(continue on reverse side if necessary)

PLEASE LIST AT LEAST THREE (3) RICKS WE MAY CONTACT AS REFERENCES:

HOT DOGS ON A RICK

 6 hot dogs   Prep: 45 minutes
Cook: 25 minutes

6 skewers 8.5 by ³⁄₁₆ inches

6 hot dogs

6 slices low-moisture mozzarella cheese

1 cup cornmeal

1 cup flour

2 tablespoons white sugar

4 teaspoons baking powder

½ teaspoon salt

½ teaspoon onion powder

1 teaspoon ancho chili powder

1 cup oil for frying

½ cup milk (more if needed)

1 egg

1   Insert skewers lengthwise through center of hot dog, leaving enough to serve as a handle, then set aside.

2   Lay down 1 piece of sliced cheese, then place hot dog horizontally across it. Wrap cheese slice around hot dog, using fingers to pinch ends of cheese together so it stays put. Repeat with remaining hot dogs and cheese. Refrigerate for 10 to 15 minutes while preparing batter.

3   Heat oil in a large Dutch oven to 350° to 375°F.

4   Combine cornmeal, flour, sugar, baking powder, salt, onion powder, ancho chili powder, milk, and egg into a large mixing bowl, then whisk together until batter comes together. Batter consistency should be similar to that of pancake batter, and batter should drip off the end of a spoon or whisk when inserted. Transfer batter to a thin container tall enough to submerge hot dogs.

5   Dip one hot dog at a time into batter and swirl 2 to 3 times to ensure even coating. Remove from batter and allow excess to drip off before placing into frying oil. Fry for 3 to 5 minutes or until golden brown. Remove and drain on a wire rack. Serve customers, making sure they have a "Hot Dog of a Day."

RICK ON A HOT DOG!!

CAULIFLOWER PORTAL MASH

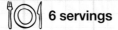 6 servings   **Prep: 30 minutes**
Cook: 15 minutes

2 heads green cauliflower, broken down

2 cloves garlic, peeled

4 cups water

1 tablespoon salt

2 tablespoons butter

½ cup vegetable broth

1 teaspoon salt

½ tablespoon lemon juice

2 tablespoons pesto (see Roasted Tomato Pesto, page 88)

2 tablespoons crema drizzled over top

OPTIONAL:

Cut up some hot dogs and arrange as a **Hot Dog Morty** just to see how it might look.

1 Break down heads of cauliflower by first removing any outer leaves, then cut off stem. With cauliflower upside down, cut florets away from inner stem, removing any leftover stem still attached to florets.

2 Set water to simmer in a medium pot, then cook florets and garlic for about 10 minutes or until tender. Remove vegetables from water, transfer to a food processor, then add butter, vegetable broth, salt, and lemon juice. Puree until mixture is smooth, then transfer to a round serving dish.

3 Using a spoon or spatula, swirl pesto around top of cauliflower mash to create the effect of Rick's portal. Finish with drizzled crema for the final touch.

So, here's another "Morty recipe" I kind of changed up myself! (For that extra credit?)

It's a CAULIFLOWER PORTAL MASH!

It's like mashed potatoes—but cauliflower! And, did you know there's green cauliflower? But it's not broccoli?

I mean, that's not the personal part. But, wow, I really am learning some stuff, while putting this book together!

So, sure, you could have boring old normal mashed potatoes—or you could try this new thing! And, hey, look—I made it look like those portals my grandpa Rick makes, you know? It's got different greens, and some little white bits? That's fun, right?

Boy, well, when I see that, there's usually some new experience on the other side. And now you can have your own new experience—a taste adventure! Ha ha.

What's wrong with NORMAL? I mean, seriously, in all the time I spent busting my ass through college, then medical school, then having and raising TWO CHILDREN while working to SUPPORT A FAMILY and SAVE LIVES, did the world decide that EVERY FOOD has to be "fusion," or something we've never even HEARD OF before?

Sometimes I just want to have one of the classic, home-cooked staples I've had since I was a kid! (Even if my own children are eye-rolling, and saying it makes us look "basic.") And sometimes, being "basic" can mean comfort and stability—while being "extra" might mean making a CLONE of your daughter and shooting one into space, but then PRETENDING LIKE IT DIDN'T HAPPEN!

ORDINARY GREEN BEAN CASSEROLE

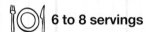 6 to 8 servings   **Prep:** 30 minutes
Cook: 45-60 minutes

4 ounces pancetta, diced

10 ounces mushrooms, chopped

1 tablespoon butter

1 small yellow onion, diced

4 tablespoons butter

¼ cup flour

1 cup whole milk

1 cup vegetable broth

One 16-ounce bag whole frozen green beans

5 ounces seasoned croutons, crushed

1   Preheat oven to 375°F.

2   In a large saucepan, sauté pancetta until crisp — about 5 minutes — then remove with a slotted spoon and set aside in a large bowl. In the remaining fat, melt 1 tablespoon butter and sauté mushrooms until browned on all sides, about 5 to 10 minutes. Once mushrooms are cooked, add onion and sauté until translucent, another 3 to 5 minutes. Once cooked, transfer to a bowl with pancetta and set aside.

3   In the same pan, melt 4 tablespoons butter until foaming, then add flour and cook, stirring constantly until raw-flour smell has worn off, about 2 to 3 minutes. Slowly add milk, whisking constantly to avoid lumps. Once milk is added, repeat this process with vegetable broth.

4   Pour sauce into the bowl with vegetables and pancetta, and add green beans, then mix until combined. Transfer mixture into a 9-by-13-inch baking pan and top evenly with croutons. Cover with foil and bake for 20 to 25 minutes, then remove foil and bake for another 10 to 15 minutes. Serve hot and enjoy!

JUST CHEESY SCALLOPED POTATOES

 6 to 8 servings

Prep: 40 minutes
Cook: 50 minutes

2 tablespoons butter

2 pounds potatoes, peeled and cut into ¼-inch slices

1½ teaspoons kosher salt

1½ teaspoons black pepper (or to taste)

3 cups cheddar cheese, grated

1¼ cup whole milk

1¼ cup half-and-half

1 egg, beaten

4 cloves garlic, diced

1   Preheat oven to 375°F.

2   Carefully cut potatoes along their length into ¼-inch-thick slices. This can be done with a knife but will be difficult. A mandoline is recommended for easy, consistent slicing.

3   Grease the bottom of a 9-by-13-inch glass baking dish with half of butter. Place single layer of potato slices on the bottom of the pan and sprinkle with ½ teaspoon of salt and pepper. Top with 1 cup of shredded cheese. Repeat this layering once more, then top with remaining slices of potato. Set aside.

4   In a small saucepan over low heat, whisk together milk, half-and-half, egg, and garlic. Bring to a gentle simmer for 1 to 2 minutes. Carefully pour this mixture into the baking dish, and sprinkle top with remaining cheese, salt, and pepper. Cut remaining butter into small pieces and dot on top of potatoes. Bake for 45 to 50 minutes until potatoes are tender but still firm.

ALTERNATE REALITY PIZZA

 6 to 8 servings   Prep: 1 hour, 15 minutes
Cook: 45 minutes

I don't know if you've ever traveled to alternate dimensions or anything (doubt it, right?), but it's amazing how many ways things can be different that just, like, open your mind in ways you never would have imagined living in this total fart-void of a town.

There are worlds without genders, or ownership, or mirrors (mixed bag), or with a kind of tea that lets you astral-project your consciousness into theme park ride, so no one has to wait in lines (but that's not OUR world, so that's sad for you). There are worlds where there's never been a war, and one where literally everyone died in a twenty-year fight over changing a college-football mascot. Makes you think, right?

Anyway, traveling has really expanded my horizons, and I like my pizza like this other world makes it, now.

One 28-ounce can crushed tomatoes

One 15-ounce can tomato sauce

One 6-ounce can tomato paste

1 teaspoon dried basil

½ teaspoon dried oregano

1 teaspoon garlic powder

½ teaspoon crushed red pepper

1 teaspoon kosher salt

1 teaspoon balsamic vinegar

Black pepper to taste

One 16-ounce package ready-to-use pizza dough

½ cup (1 stick) butter, melted

1 teaspoon garlic powder

6 ounces grated Parmesan cheese

8 ounces shredded low-moisture mozzarella

One 6-ounce bag pepperoni slices

EQUIPMENT

Bundt pan

1. In a pot, over medium heat, combine crushed tomatoes, tomato sauce, tomato paste, basil, oregano, garlic powder, and crushed red pepper. Stir to incorporate, then bring to a gentle simmer.

2. Add salt and balsamic vinegar; season with black pepper to taste. Simmer very low for 25 to 30 minutes, stirring frequently to avoid burning and bubbling over. Once done, set aside off the heat and begin creating pizza.

3. Preheat oven to 425°F.

4. In a microwave-safe bowl, melt butter and whisk in garlic powder. This will create a glaze for pizza dough. Using a brush or paper towel, grease bundt pan with some of this mixture.

5. Place single layer of whole pepperoni slices in the bottom of the greased bundt pan, then slice remainder of pepperoni into ribbons. (This will make it easier to pull apart later.) Cover pepperoni with ¼ cup shredded mozzarella and ½ cup pizza sauce. Spread evenly. Set aside and begin working with pizza dough.

6. Working on a floured surface, break off small pieces of dough and roll into 1½- to- 2-inch balls. Coat each ball in garlic-butter mixture, then roll in grated Parmesan, before placing coated dough balls in a single layer in the bundt pan.

7. Once first layer of dough has been placed, coat with another ½ cup of pizza sauce, followed by ¼ cup of shredded mozzarella, then ¼ cup pepperoni ribbons. Repeat this process with remainder of ingredients. Cover the top of the bundt pan with foil and bake for 25 to 30 minutes.

8. Once dough has puffed nicely, remove foil to crisp top 5 to 10 minutes.

9. Remove from the oven and allow to cool for 10 to 15 minutes. Carefully invert the bundt pan onto a large plate and remove cooked ingredients. Serve with remaining pizza sauce for dipping.

Hey, Mom

I know this might sound weird, but I just lived sixty-plus years of simulated life ("Roy"), and . . . it felt REAL. I lost all sense of time, and of myself.

I grew from a childhood in someone else's home to being the patriarch of a family I now know I'll never really have. I experienced his joys and sensations. His heartbreaks and disappointments were mine, too.

Ultimately, when it ended, it was a sharp and sudden ejection into objective PROOF that the life I just lived had literally meant nothing. And then I started to worry that maybe the same is true for "my" life—or all of ours—if people like Rick are right about the universe . . .

So, I've kind of been spiraling out for the last few days. The trick is, I keep going to stuff that might make me feel better—hobbies, favorite music, comfort food, stuff like that—but then I realize I'm going for stuff that made ROY feel better. But that's not me. And then I start to spiral out all over again.

I'm trying to remind myself who MORTY is. And reconnect with all the stuff that I loved from MY life! And that brings me to this.

THIS is the exception. The way you make meat loaf sucks, and Roy's mom's is way better. And luckily, I made it enough times in the game that I remember the recipe. Please burn your old recipe and use this for the future instead.

Your son (I think! Unless this universe is a simulation, too! Ha ha!),

Morty

ROY'S MEAT LOAF

 6 to 8 servings **Prep:** 45 minutes
Cook: 45 minutes

FOR MEAT LOAF:

1 tablespoon vegetable oil

1 yellow onion, diced

3 carrots, diced

2 celery sticks, diced

½ teaspoon dried oregano

1 pound ground beef

1 pound ground turkey

½ cup bread crumbs

2 tablespoons Worcestershire sauce

½ teaspoon garlic powder

1 egg

FOR MEAT LOAF GLAZE:

1 cup ketchup

1 tablespoon Worcestershire sauce

2 tablespoons Dijon mustard

1 tablespoon apple cider vinegar

1 tablespoon dark molasses

1 Heat oil in a large frying pan. Sauté onion, carrots, celery, and dried oregano until onions are translucent, then set aside and allow to cool to room temperature.

2 Preheat oven to 375°F.

3 While vegetables are cooling, in a large bowl, combine beef, turkey, bread crumbs, Worcestershire sauce, garlic powder, and egg. Add vegetables once they are cool, and fully incorporate using hands to create an emulsified mixture. Transfer meat loaf into a 9-by-13-inch glass baking dish and shape into a uniform rectangle. Set aside while preparing glaze.

4 In a bowl, combine all glaze ingredients and whisk thoroughly. Pour about half of the glaze on top of meat loaf, then use a brush to spread evenly on all sides. Add remaining half of glaze to a small saucepan and heat on low for about 3 to 5 minutes until just simmering. Serve on the side with finished meat loaf.

5 Bake for 30 to 45 minutes until the internal temperature reaches 165°F. Remove from oven and allow to cool for 5 minutes before serving with extra glaze.

NEEDFUL THINGS

SUMMER! My faithful employee, and ye of little faith. I have, for you, an item I know you have longed for . . . endless meals from the WHOLESOME DELIGHTS menu!

Of course, you undoubtedly had hoped I would grant you regular vegan luncheon delivery on your shifts. Or perhaps some "lifetime of meals" contest victory? But when I attempted to strike a bargain with "Doug" the "franchisee" and inquired as to what he most desired, the answer was the one thing I was not expecting . . .

MONEY.

Unfortunately, having built my own business on a payment system of tragic ironies and moral corruption, I am a bit short on actual financial assets at the moment. (It seemed tragic irony had its eye on ME!) But then, of course, I remembered I am quite the literal little Devil—and merely convinced the proprietor to burn down his storefront for the insurance money.

But not before I absconded with some of their specialty recipes! I deliver them to you as a token of my appreciation. (I recognize the irony that your gift from work, when hoping for a delightful and healthy vegan treat, is that you will now have to work MORE to make it yourself. But I really didn't mean it as a curse or anything. It's just one of those crappy, bitter indignities of life in an imperfect world that made me rebel against God in the heavens and His casual disdain for the tediousness of the existence he hath wrought.)

Bon appetit!

KALE SALAD

 6 TO 8 SERVINGS   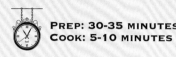 PREP: 30-35 MINUTES
COOK: 5-10 MINUTES

FOR ROASTED CHICKPEAS:

15.5-ounce can of chickpeas

1 tablespoon olive oil

½ teaspoon kosher salt

½ teaspoon curry powder

FOR DRESSING:

¼ cup rice vinegar

¼ cup olive oil

2 tablespoons Dijon mustard

2 tablespoons brown sugar

2 to 3 cloves of garlic, diced

FOR SALAD:

1 bunch dino kale

1 tablespoon olive oil

1 teaspoon salt

1 cucumber, peeled and deseeded

1 cup corn kernels

8 ounces cherry tomatoes, halved

1 red bell pepper, sliced

4 stalks green onion, sliced thin

Prepared chickpeas

Prepared dressing

1 Mix in a sealable jar and shake together.

2 Preheat oven to 400°F.

3 Drain chickpeas and pat very dry. (Liquid can be saved to make Riggity, Riggity Ranch, page 35.) Transfer to a rimmed baking sheet and coat with olive oil, curry powder, and salt. Roast for 5 to 10 minutes until crispy. Set aside to cool.

4 While chickpeas are cooling, combine dressing ingredients into a container with a very good seal. (A mason jar works well.) Shake dressing until combined, usually 30 seconds to 1 minute, then set aside. Dressing will naturally separate; shake again to emulsify.

5 Remove kale leaves from stem by holding end of stem in one hand. With the other hand pinching just above the leaves, pull your fingers down length of stem to strip leaves. Slice leaves into ribbons, then place into a bowl with olive oil and salt. Massage kale and allow to rest for at least 10 minutes.

6 Combine cucumber, corn, tomatoes, bell pepper, green onion, and chickpeas in the bowl with kale and mix to combine. Drizzle with desired amount of dressing, toss, and enjoy.

ROASTED ACORN SQUASH SOUP

 6 TO 8 SERVINGS PREP: 45 MINUTES
COOK: 1 HOUR

FOR SOUP:

2 to 3 acorn squash, cut in
half and seeded

½ tablespoon olive oil
(to spread on squash)

1 teaspoon salt

1 tablespoon butter

1 tablespoon olive oil

1 shallot, finely minced

½ cup vegetable stock

1 sprig rosemary

⅓ cup white wine

FOR TOPPING:

½ cup raw pumpkin seeds

1 tablespoon unsalted
butter

¼ teaspoon kosher salt

¼ teaspoon paprika

1   Preheat oven to 450°F.

2   Place squash skin side down on a rimmed baking sheet and
coat with olive oil and salt. Bake for 30 to 35 minutes until
flesh is tender and can be pierced easily with a fork.

3   While squash is roasting, melt butter in a frying pan and fry
pumpkin seeds for about 3 to 5 minutes until toasted. After
pumpkin seeds are cooked, transfer to a bowl and toss with
salt and paprika. Set aside for soup topping.

4   Once squash is cooked, remove from the oven and allow to
cool completely before scooping flesh into a bowl. Discard
skins and set squash aside.

5   In a large pot, heat butter and olive oil on medium. Once
butter is foaming, sauté shallot until translucent. Add reserved
squash and remove from heat. Using an immersion blender,
or working in batches with a standing blender, incorporate
vegetable stock.

6   After blending mixture, return the pot to medium-low heat.
(If using a standing blender, transfer back into the pot and
return to heat.) Add white wine and rosemary sprig.
Cook for another 10 to 15 minutes until the smell of raw
alcohol has gone away.

7   Top with toasted pumpkin seeds and enjoy.

MINESTRONE SOUP

 6 TO 8 SERVINGS **PREP: 45 MINUTES**
COOK: 45 MINUTES

16 ounces ditalini noodles

2 tablespoons vegetable oil

1 large yellow onion, diced

2 carrots, sliced into rounds

3 celery sticks, sliced thin

3 cloves garlic, minced

1 teaspoon dried thyme leaves

¼ teaspoon rosemary leaves, dry

1 teaspoon kosher salt

One 6-ounce can tomato paste

One 28-ounce can diced tomatoes

4 Yukon Gold potatoes, peeled and diced

2 zucchinis, deseeded and diced

10 ounces green beans cut into small pieces

1 bay leaf

64 ounces vegetable stock

1 Let simmer for 5 to 10 minutes, then add one box ditalini pasta noodles and cook to package instructions.

2 In a large stockpot, heat oil on medium and sauté onion, celery, carrot, garlic, garlic, thyme, and rosemary. Cook for 3 to 5 minutes until onions are translucent. Once onions are ready, add tomato paste and sauté another 3 minutes. Stir in diced tomatoes and simmer for another 10 minutes.

3 Add potato, zucchini, and green beans. Toss in bay leaf and cover with vegetable stock. Stir everything together until combined and simmer for another 20 to 25 minutes. Add noodles and cook according to package instructions.

4 Season with salt and pepper to taste. Enjoy.

ROASTED TOMATO PESTO

 6 TO 8 SERVINGS **PREP: 35 MINUTES**
COOK: 35-40 MINUTES

16 ounces cherry tomatoes, sliced in half

¼ cup olive oil

1 teaspoon kosher salt

black pepper to taste

⅓ cup walnuts, roasted

½ cup grated Parmesan cheese, with more for topping

3 cloves of garlic

2 cups fresh basil leaves

½ cup olive oil

½ teaspoon balsamic vinegar

¼ cup pasta water for pesto sauce

16 ounces linguine noodle (or any wide, flat noodle)

1 Preheat oven to 350°F.

2 Combine tomato halves, oil, salt, and pepper on a rimmed baking sheet. Roast for 20 to 25 minutes until soft and some brown spots have appeared. Remove from the oven and set aside to cool.

3 In a food processor, combine walnuts and garlic. Pulse for 1 to 2 minutes until it resembles wet sand. Add Parmesan cheese and pulse together briefly. Add basil a handful at a time, and pulse until well combined before adding the next handful.

4 To emulsify pesto, set the food processor to run continuously and then slowly pour olive oil into mixture for proper emulsification. Continue until all olive oil is used, then add in balsamic vinegar, give it one last pulse, and set aside while pasta is cooked.

5 Cook pasta in a large pot according to package instructions, drain (reserving ¼ cup pasta water), and return pasta to pot off heat. Transfer pesto from the food processor onto pasta and stir to combine, using reserved pasta water to help pesto coat pasta.

6 Add in oven-roasted tomatoes and mix.

7 Pour pasta into a bowl, dust with Parmesan cheese, and serve.

LEGAL DISCLAIMER OR SOMETHING LIKE THAT!

So, yeah, these recipes were provided by a guy who might be the Devil. He's at least vaguely something like that while still fitting into whatever science or cosmology or whatever. Anyway, point is, MAKE THOSE LAST COUPLE RECIPES AT YOUR OWN RISK. They might have secret ironic curses in there somehow. I don't know—I haven't tried making them.

But mostly because it looks like too much work.

Hi, son.

Still not responding to emails, I guess. Are kids these days "so over" email? Is your old man just not "on fleek" for using the old electronic letter to keep in touch?

Well, I know once you miss Dear Old Dad, you'll be able to crack open the old account and pick up some of that fatherly advice you might be taking for granted as a kid. (I won't ALWAYS be here, you know!)

So, since I'm probably talking to FUTURE Morty, I figured maybe I'll start sharing some "adulting" tips! And lucky for you, I just enrolled in an adult education course—in cooking! (Thought I might meet some swinging young singles, like me—but everyone ELSE in the class turned out to be sad, old losers. FACE-PALM, right?)

But without further ado, here's my favorite so far—POT PIE FOR ONE! A delicious and nutritious all-in-one meal for a guy who's ALSO great "all by himself". (And a total "SNACK," as the kids say.)

And I'm gonna keep the hits coming! Up next: How to save on your bills by maxing out your community center membership!

JERRY'S SINGLES POT PIE

 6 pot pies   **Prep: 1 hour, 10 minutes**
Cook: 45 minutes

INGREDIENTS! :-)

FOR BISCUITS:

2 cups flour, with ½ cup reserved to coat surface and hands

2 tablespoons powdered buttermilk

1¼ teaspoons baking powder

1 teaspoon kosher salt

¾ teaspoon sugar

⅛ teaspoon baking soda

½ cup (1 stick) butter, cut into small pieces and chilled

1 tablespoon butter, melted, for brushing

½ cup cold water

FOR POT PIE FILLING:

1 tablespoon vegetable oil

3 carrots, sliced thin

3 stalks of celery, sliced thin

1 medium yellow onion, diced

8 ounces mushrooms, diced

1½ pounds boneless skinless chicken thighs, cut into 1-inch cubes

½ teaspoon kosher salt

Black pepper to taste

1 teaspoon fresh rosemary, finely minced

2 tablespoons Dijon mustard

1 cup frozen peas

¼ cup flour

1 cup vegetable stock

TO MAKE BISCUITS:

1 Preheat the oven to 400°F.

2 Place flour, powdered buttermilk, baking powder, salt, sugar, and baking soda in a large bowl and mix thoroughly.

3 Add chilled butter pieces. Use a pastry cutter to mix until remaining butter pieces are pea-size. Slowly pour in cold water and mix with a fork until a shaggy ball of dough forms. Transfer dough to a clean, flat surface and shape into a 1-inch-thick square.

4 Using a knife, cut dough into 4 equal pieces and stack them. Roll this stack into a 1-inch-thick rectangle.

5 Using a round biscuit cutter, cut 6 biscuits out of dough and place on a parchment-lined baking sheet, then freeze for 10 to 15 minutes.

NOTE: Biscuits can be frozen uncovered until solid, then transferred to a bag or container and kept for about 1 month. Do not thaw before baking.

TO MAKE FILLING:

6 Heat vegetable oil in the bottom of a Dutch oven on medium heat. Once oil is hot, add carrots, celery, and onion. Saute 3 to 5 minutes or until onion is translucent. Remove from the pot and set aside. If you would like to make this a vegetarian pot pie, add mushrooms in with other veggies and skip chicken. Other steps are consistent.

7 Add chicken to the Dutch oven and season with salt and pepper. Cook chicken on all sides for about 5 to 7 minutes. Once chicken is cooked, make a well in the center and pour Dijon mustard, add rosemary, and cook for another 3 to 5 minutes. Add peas and previously cooked vegetables, then stir to combine.

8 Coat filling in flour and stir together for 1 to 2 minutes before slowly adding vegetable stock, stirring another 1 to 2 minutes until no flour clumps remain.

9 Deposit filling into six oven-safe bowls, about 1¼ cups of filling to each bowl. Top each with 1 biscuit and brush with butter.

10 Bake for 20 to 25 minutes until golden brown.

Subject: PERFECT GRILLED CHEESE RECIPE

HEY JERRY, it's JERRY! Just preserving for all time that you did it, you GLORIOUS Bastard! (And take THAT, Quentin Tarantino!) After your millionth time farting around making a grilled cheese, IT CAME OUT BETTER THAN SEX!

(And in case someone else is reading my emails to myself, my sex is perfectly good, thank you—and GET OUT OF MY EMAIL! (NO thank you!)

And for ONCE, Rick's weird inventions did something GOOD—with Butter Robot's camera catching the whole experiment! So, here's a reconstruction or transcript or something for future replication/possible contest submissions (?!?) WHO'S THE GREAT INVENTOR NOW??!

JERRY'S GRILLED CHEESE

 1 sandwich   **Prep: 15 minutes**
Cook: 10 minutes

INGREDIENTS! :-)

2 slices sourdough bread

½ tablespoon butter

2 slices pepper jack cheese

2 to 3 slices pack Black Forest ham

8 ounces asiago cheese, shredded

1 large vine tomato, thinly sliced

HOW TO MAKE IT :-o

1   Lightly toast bread slices for structure. Butter one side of each slice, then lightly press 1 tablespoon of shredded cheese onto each buttered side of toast.

2   Place one slice of bread, cheese, and butter face down into a frying pan on medium heat.

3   Cook for 1 to 3 minutes until cheese has melted into bread and begun to brown slightly.

4   Begin building your sandwich in the pan by placing a slice of pepper jack on bare toast, followed by tomato, ham, cheese, and, finally, the other piece of toast, buttered side up.

5   Flip sandwich and cook for another 1 to 3 minutes until cheese on the bottom has crisped and pepper jack inside is melted.

6   Transfer to a plate, slice into triangles, and serve warm.

Subject: The Man of the House

I'm happy to admit I'm more a "father" and "husband" and "student of life" than I am a "cook." But I love to toss on a good novelty apron and step up to the PLATE (get it?) for three particular things: the grill, the Thanksgiving turkey, and the Christmas ham!

But my father-in-law keeps "modifying" the grill to lock down at my facial recognition, and because of his weird relationship with the president, any attempts to have turkey in our house at Thanksgiving is considered a terrorist plot.

So, that leaves me with the ham. Luckily, this recipe is 100 percent Jerry Smith, and my family loves it!

JERRY'S CHRISTMAS HAM GLAZE

 Glaze for 1 spiral ham

 Prep: 5-10 minutes
Cook: 10 minutes

INGREDIENTS! :-)

> NOPE. Sorry, Jer. I hacked your recipe.
> ½ cup Mr. Beauregard's Memory Marmalade
> Remember Mr. Beauregard? He was FAKE, and
> we all like his cooking better than yours!

> **OPTIONAL**
> 2 tablespoons bourbon. I mean, you could leave that out. And personally, I'll be pouring on way more. But I'm just trying to up your game here.

¼ cup fresh orange juice

¼ teaspoon allspice

¼ teaspoon Chinese five spice powder

HOW TO MAKE IT :-D

1 In a small saucepan, combine marmalade, orange juice, allspice, and Chinese five spice powder over medium-low heat. Gently whisk to combine, and simmer for 5 to 10 minutes or until thickened. Set aside and glaze ham during the last 20 minutes of cooking.

> You can also drink the rest of the bourbon while you wait. If you set a timer or something for the food, that'll probably wake you if you pass out. Or the smoke alarm will.

COURAGEOUS CHILI DOGS

 6 chili dogs

 Prep: 30-35 minutes
Cook: 1 hour, 15 minutes or more

INGREDIENTS! :-)

FOR CHILI:

1 pound ground beef

1 yellow onion, diced

One 1.4-ounce can diced green chilies

2 serrano peppers, seeded

3 cloves garlic, crushed or finely minced

One 6-ounce can tomato paste

1 teaspoon chili powder

1 teaspoon ancho chili

1 teaspoon ground cumin

¼ teaspoon white pepper

1 cup light beer

One 15-ounce can crushed tomatoes

One 29-ounce can tomato sauce

One 15-ounce can red kidney beans

2 tablespoons apple cider vinegar

FOR CHILI DOGS:

6 hot dog buns, toasted

6 hot dogs, cooked according to your choice

Prepared chili

½ red onion, diced small for topping

1 cup shredded cheddar cheese for topping

HOW TO MAKE IT :-o

1 In a large pot on medium heat, brown and break up ground beef until it has cooked 3 to 5 minutes. Add diced onion, green chili, serranos, and garlic, then sauté for another 2 to 3 minutes until onions are translucent. Add tomato paste, chili powder, ancho chili, ground cumin, and white pepper, continue to sauté while stirring frequently for 5 minutes.

2 Pour in light beer and simmer for 7 to 10 minutes until beer is reduced by half. Once beer has reduced, add crushed tomatoes, tomato sauce, beans, and vinegar. Stir to combine and simmer on medium-low heat for at least 1 hour, stirring occasionally to prevent burning. If darker and more reduced chili is desired, continue to simmer until desired color is achieved.

TO ASSEMBLE CHILI DOGS:

3 Cook hot dogs with preferred method. Nestle each cooked hot dog into toasted bun, top with ½ cup of prepared chili, then sprinkle with cheese and onions as desired. Serve with several napkins.

COURAGE

DESSERTS

OOOO-WEEE! I sure do love a tasty little treat, don't you?

I'm Mr. Poopybutthole, remember me?

And I think we all deserve to enjoy the desserts in life! Too many days turn sour, am I right? But maybe an extra bit of sweetness can keep US from turning bitter! Oooh-wee.

Like that one time Beth shot me, back in season two? There were some days when I was learning to walk again where my head was so full of anger and hopelessness that I wondered if I'd have been better off bleeding to death! OOOO-WEE!

But by the time a recovery nurse was spoon-feeding me some pudding? That little kick of chocolate almost made me forget my whole life had just been derailed! Almost . . .

Anyway, I bet there's some real good treats in here that could help YOU forget whatever's goin' on with you . . . maybe stuck in a job that makes you miserable, but you're too scared of total uncertainty to quit? Or feelin' trapped in a relationship that's become something you never would've chosen? Maybe it just feels like death keeps circling all around and you can't be left alone with your own thoughts without fixating on how eternal oblivion could just snatch us up at any moment, but you know worryin' about it isn't making you live life any fuller—it's just paralyzing you with fear and regret! Ooooooooo-weeee . . .

Sounds like you could use some dessert!

KALAXIAN CRYSTALS

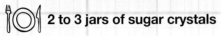 2 to 3 jars of sugar crystals

 Prep: 25 minutes
Cook: 15 minutes

Dear, umm . . . Morty's Teacher. I know your "honorable" PROFESSION loathes sugar, as it makes it more difficult for you to fill young minds with your useless drivel, but I'm here to tell you to . . . suck it! And by "it," I obviously mean my delicious Kalaxian Crystals! Ha ha! See what I did there?

1 cup water

Skewers

3 cups sugar, plus 1 tablespoon for rolling skewers

Clothespins

Mason jar, cleaned

3 to 4 drops pink food coloring (or color of choice)

½ teaspoon food-grade essential oil (flavor of choice)

Coffee filter

Rubber band

1   Wet skewer with water, then roll in granulated sugar, leaving at least 2 inches bare to use as a handle. Set aside to dry completely. This will form a place for crystals to start growing.

2   Fasten a clothespin horizontally across the bare end of the skewer. Rest the skewer in the jar such that the clothespin spans the top of the jar. If the skewer reaches the bottom of the jar, make sure to trim it or crystal will get stuck to the bottom.

3   In a medium saucepan on medium high heat, bring water to a boil. Add ½ cup of sugar at a time, stirring until completely dissolved before adding next ½ cup. Once sugar no longer dissolves, mixture is ready. Add food coloring until desired shade is reached, and stir in essential oil as well.

4   Carefully pour hot sugar solution into jar until the skewer is covered. Top with a coffee filter and fasten with a rubber band to avoid dust and critters that may want to steal crystals. Allow mixture to cool before moving to a cool, dry place out of direct sunlight.

5   Crystals take about 7 days to fully form. If a layer of crystal has built up around the top of the jar, gently break with a spoon before removing grown crystals.

6   Once grown, transfer crystal to an empty glass and allow to drip-dry. Enjoy responsibly!

ROY'S CELEBRATION CAKE

 8 to 10 servings

Prep: 1 hour, 30 minutes
Cook: 45 minutes

FOR CAKE:

3 cups flour

2¼ teaspoons baking powder

¾ teaspoon baking soda

¼ tsp salt

1 cup (2 sticks) unsalted butter

2¼ cups sugar

1 tablespoon vanilla extract

4 eggs

½ cup milk

1 cup Greek yogurt

FOR FROSTING:

2 tablespoons meringue powder

⅓ cup water

6 cups sifted powdered sugar, divided

1¼ sticks unsalted butter, softened, cut into tablespoon-size chunks

¼ teaspoon salt

1 teaspoon vanilla extract

Pink food coloring

¼ cup of milk

¼ cup chopped dried pineapple slices, plus more for decoration

¼ cup chopped natural cocktail cherries, plus more for decoration

HAPPY REGISTERED BIRTH / HATCHING / FORMATION DAY

FROM YOUR FRIENDS AT **Blips AND Chitz**

According to our tracking of all your activities, preferences, and in-game choices stored on your Blips & Chitz Play Pass, we thought you might want to celebrate your special occasion with ROY'S CELEBRATION CAKE!

Straight from the most complete full-life simulator game in the universe, this recipe will let you recreate the taste as you experienced it, based on your life-form type and planetary origin!

And when you're done celebrating at home, come back to any Blips & Chitz location with this card, to receive TWO FREE CREDITS PLAY!**

From your friends*** at Blips & Chitz

1   Prepare two 8-inch cake pans by lining the bottoms with parchment.

2   In a medium bowl, mix flour, baking powder, baking soda, and salt together and have standing by.

3   In the bowl of a stand mixer fitted with a paddle attachment, beat butter and sugar together until light and fluffy. Add eggs, one at a time, scraping down the sides after each addition.

4   Add vanilla.

5   Mix milk with Greek yogurt.

6   Starting with about ⅓ of dry mixture, alternate between dry and yogurt mixtures. Mix well and scrape down the bowl after each addition.

7   Divide batter evenly between the 2 pans and bake for 30 to 35 minutes or until a cake tester comes out clean. Rotate cakes halfway through the cooking time.

8   Allow to cool on a wire rack for 15 minutes. Using an offset spatula, gently work it between cake and the pan to loosen the edge and then turn out cake onto the wire rack to cool completely.

TO MAKE FROSTING:

9   In the bowl of a stand mixer with the whisk attachment, combine meringue powder and water. Whip at high speed until peaks form. Add 4 cups of powdered sugar, 1 cup at a time, mixing well after each addition.

10 Alternate between butter pieces and remaining sugar until all is incorporated. Add salt and vanilla extract and beat on low speed until smooth.

11 If using immediately, let stand at room temperature. To store, transfer to an airtight container and refrigerate for up to 1 week. Allow to come to room temperature before using.

12 Take about 2 cups of buttercream, reserve the rest, and mix in chopped fruit.

13 Place cake layer on a cake stand and frost with buttercream-fruit mixture. Spread smooth.

14 Stack second layer on top of first.

15 Dilute remaining buttercream with small amounts of milk until mixture is the consistency of a thin batter.

16 Starting in center of cake, pour frosting on and gently push with an offset spatula until frosting just begins to drip down side.

17 Reserve extra frosting in the refrigerator for future use.

18 Decorate with additional pineapple slices cut in half, and add 2 stemmed cherries.

STRAWBERRIES ON A COB

 8 to 10 servings

 Prep: 30 minutes
Cook: 45 minutes

You know what's fun? Things on cobs! Why limit it to just corn?

When my family was on the run from the Galactic Federation and forced to abandon our entire lives, support systems, and PLANET with the constant threat of torture, dismemberment, and death constantly hanging over our heads (AAAAGGHH!!!!)—the one little happy surprise that made my kids smile was stumbling onto a world with strawberries on a cob!

Everything else there was too, unfortunately. So the novelty quickly turned into the dread that the forces of the planet would eventually meld our family together into some sort of horrifying "Human Centipede"-esque HUMANS on a Cob. (To be clear—we left before that could happen.)

But! When trying to stop my kids from spiraling out into catastrophic depression, with their lives and futures ripped away from them, I decided to whip up my OWN version of Strawberries on a Cob as a special treat, hoping we could look back and laugh!

They just started screaming and crying again. And my dad destroyed them with chemical fire. (Thought we "brought invasive flora.") But I can't stand letting all that work go to waste.

SO YOU BETTER MAKE AND ENJOY THIS WHIMSICAL TREAT, DAMN IT!

½ cup all-purpose flour

¼ teaspoon baking soda

1 teaspoon baking powder

¾ cup half-and-half

¼ cup sour cream

1 teaspoon vanilla paste or extract

½ cup pulverized freeze-dried strawberries

½ cup (1 stick) butter, room temperature

1 cup sugar

2 eggs

FOR CREAM CHEESE FROSTING:

8 ounces cream cheese, softened

½ cup butter (1 stick), softened

4 cups powdered sugar

Zest of 1 lemon

Juice of 1 lemon

1 to 2 drops green food coloring

FOR ASSEMBLY:

18 cake pop sticks

9 green-apple fruit leather rolls

2 ounces freeze-dried strawberry slices

2 bags (20 ounces) white chocolate melts

1. Preheat the oven to 350°F.

2. Whisk flour, baking soda, and baking powder together in a bowl; set aside. In another bowl, combine half-and-half, sour cream, vanilla, and pulverized strawberries; set the mixture aside to allow strawberries to rehydrate.

3. In the bowl of a stand mixer, beat butter until light and fluffy. Slowly add sugar and continue beating until mixture is pale. Add 1 egg at a time, fully incorporating before adding next egg.

4. Begin adding flour mixture and the strawberry mixture to mixing bowl on low speed, about ½ cup at a time, alternating.

5. Pour batter into a 9-by-13-inch baking pan and bake for 40 to 45 minutes or until a cake tester comes out clean. Remove cake from the oven and poke holes across surface. Allow to cool.

6. Add lemon juice and zest. Mix again until incorporated, blending in last cup of powdered sugar until completely smooth. Reserve 1 cup and refrigerate the rest.

7. Crumble cake into a large bowl. Add remaining ¼ cup pulverized dried strawberries and 1 cup frosting, then mix with spatula or wooden spoon until combined. Refrigerate for 10 minutes.

8. Working on a parchment-lined cookie sheet, scoop ¼ cup of cake pop mixture. Form cake around each stick in the shape of a cob of corn. Repeat with remaining mixture to make about 18 cake pops.

9. Freeze for at least 30 minutes before coating with remaining frosting.

10. Melt chocolate in a heatproof bowl in microwave about 15 seconds at a time to avoid burning. Once chocolate is fully melted, coat each cake pop in a layer of melted chocolate and allow to harden at room temperature. Unroll fruit sheet and cut into 6 irregular triangular slices "husk" on cobs. Place 3 strips at base of cob and pinch onto the stick, then curl into desired shape. Decorate as desired.

11. Freeze cake pops for 5 to 10 more minutes to set. Enjoy!

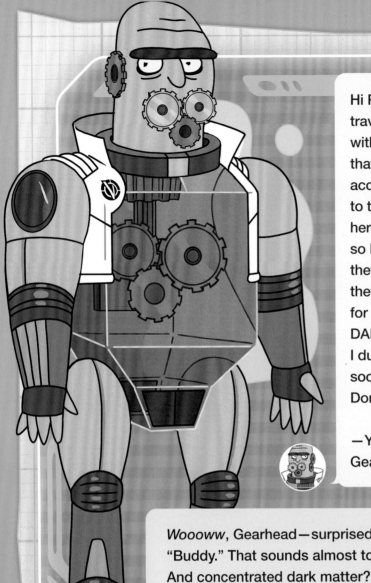

Hi Rick its me, your friend Gearhead. I was traveling to Gazorpazorp and got stranded without my phone or wallet or anything! (So thats why Im contacting you from a new account no other reason and dont reach out to the old ones.) But the police are holding me here because I cant pay or prove who I am so I need you to PLEASE SEND HELP. Except they wont take money or anything, they said they will let me go if I can get them a recipe for brownies that contain CONCENTRATED DARK MATTER. I guess thats what they eat? I dunno—HAHAHA so weird. Please send as soon as you can or they will cut off my arms! Dont think just send!!

—Your friend
Gearhead

Woooww, Gearhead—surprised to hear from you, "Buddy." That sounds almost too crazy to believe . . . And concentrated dark matter? Funny, that's also the fuel for accelerated space travel. Real, uh . . . crazy coincidence there. I also know some incredibly dumb, dingleberry-looking aliens called Zigerions who constantly come after me for the same stuff with pathetically transparent scams. But I'm sure this can't be them, because it's you, my "good friend" Gearhead! So, here's a perfect recipe that just so happens to contain concentrated dark matter—and definitely no ingredients that would mix so badly with Zigerion DNA as to cause a mini-black hole in their intestines and deservedly shove them up their own asses. That won't happen at all!

Enjoy your freedom!—"Your" "Friend" "Rick"

DARK MATTER BROWNIES

 20 to 24 brownies

 Prep: 25 minutes
Cook: 30 minutes

BROWNIE BATTER:

4 ounces unsweetened baking chocolate, chopped

¾ cup butter

1½ cups white sugar

½ cup brown sugar

2 eggs

1 egg yolk

1 teaspoon vanilla extract

1 cup flour

1 cup dark chocolate chips

FOR GANACHE TOPPING:

4 ounces semisweet chocolate, chopped

2 tablespoons heavy cream

Green and pink sprinkles for decoration

1   Preheat the oven to 350°F.

2   In a large glass mixing bowl, combine butter and chopped chocolate. Microwave for 2 minutes, then stir together until butter and chocolate are both melted and smooth.

3   Stir in sugar and mix thoroughly. Mix in eggs, yolk, and vanilla until combined. Add flour and chocolate chips and mix until combined, making sure to scrape the sides and bottom of the bowl.

4   Transfer to a parchment-lined 9-by-13-inch baking pan and bake for 30 to 35 minutes until the cake tester comes out with fudgy crumbs. Remove from the oven and poke holes all over surface using a fork. Allow to cool while making ganache topping.

5   In another glass mixing bowl, combine chocolate chips and heavy cream. Microwave on high for 1 minute, then remove and let stand for another minute without disturbing. Chocolate should be melted. Whisk mixture until glossy and smooth.

6   Pour over brownies and spread into a smooth layer with an offset spatula.

7   Brownies will be done when chocolate topping has cooled and hardened, about 20 to 25 minutes. Can be placed in the refrigerator to speed up the process.

8   Once brownies have cooled, using the parchment as handles, remove from the baking pan and cut into squares. Brownies can be stored in an airtight container at room temperature. Chocolate topping is stable.

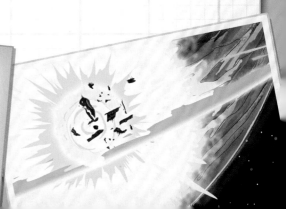

BONUS: Dark Matter Recipe!
Two parts plutonic quarks
One part cesium
And a bottle of water.

RICK'S SIMPLE WAFERS

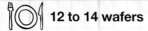 12 to 14 wafers   Prep: 4 hours, 30 minutes minimum
Cook: 25 mintues

FOR WAFER DOUGH:
1 cup (2 sticks) butter, softened
1½ cup sugar
2 eggs
3 teaspoons vanilla
3 cups flour
2 teaspoons baking powder

2 tablespoons milk
1 to 3 drops pink food coloring

FOR WAFER FILLING:
½ cup unsalted butter, softened
2 cups powdered sugar, sifted
1½ teaspoons vanilla extract
2 tablespoons milk

1 to 2 drops very light green
food coloring

TOOLS:
Wafer iron
Ice cream cone maker
Mixer

1 Cream butter and sugar together for 3 to 5 minutes or until completely incorporated.

2 Add 1 egg at a time, mixing thoroughly before adding next egg. Add vanilla once all eggs are incorporated.

3 Sift flour and baking powder into a separate bow. Slowly add to butter, sugar, and egg mixture, approximately ⅓ at a time, allowing to fully incorporate between steps. Once all flour is incorporated, add milk and food coloring.

4 Refrigerate dough for at least 4 hours. Overnight is preferred.

TO MAKE USING A WAFER IRON:

5 Place wafer iron onto the stove with the iron closed and heat on medium low. After 5 to 10 minutes, use a paper towel to gently grease the iron on both sides with butter. Close again.

6 Scoop out 1 tablespoon of dough. Roll into a ball, then press between palms to shape into a disk. Open the iron and place disk in the center, closing the wafer iron quickly and applying pressure the whole time. Cook for 1 to 2 minutes on each side. Carefully remove from the iron to place on a cutting board.

7 Cut each wafer into rectangles. Set on a wire rack to cool.

TO MAKE USING CONVENTIONAL OVEN:

8 Preheat the oven to 400°F.

9 Working on a well-floured surface, roll out wafer dough to about ⅛ of an inch thick, or as thin as possible without tearing. Using a knife or pastry cutter, cut dough into rectangles about the size of a finished wafer. Place on a cookie sheet, making sure to leave room between pieces, as they will spread. Bake for 6 to 8 minutes until golden on the edge.

TO MAKE FROSTING:

10 Cream butter in a mixer using the paddle attachment for 2 to 3 minutes until butter is smooth and fluffy. Gradually add powdered sugar ½ cup at a time, making sure to fully mix each scoop before adding more.

11 Add milk and vanilla extract, then beat for another 3 to 5 minutes until stiff. Add food coloring and mix for 20 to 30 seconds

TO ASSEMBLE WAFERS:

12 Take two finished rectangles and spread them with a generous amount of frosting in an even layer, making sure to be delicate so as not to break wafer. Sandwich second wafer on top. Repeat with remaining wafers and filling.

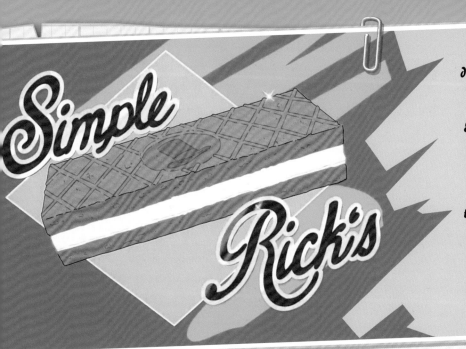

Simple Rick's

Inside a kitchen orbiting a distant star, one Rick experimented more with sugar and vanilla than plutonium and strontium-90.

Eventually, that Rick discovered a recipe for a little slice of happiness—a light wafer cookie with all the sweetness and promise of a young daughter's love.

Now, with the sun having set on the Citadel of Ricks, and the business that Rick built from scratch, the recipe can be yours.

Come home to the impossible flavor of your own completion. Come home to SIMPLE RICK'S.

MR. NIMBUS'S BEIGNETS

🍽️ 12 to 14 beignets

⏱️ Prep: 1 hour, 30 minutes
Cook: 30 minutes

Hello, Richard

I am just making sure that you and your family are prepared for the great honor and unlimited erotic potential of hosting His Majesty, King of the Oceans, Mr. Nimbus.

While there is some latitude in what meals may be appropriate and deserving of He Who Rules Two-Thirds of Earth's Surface (NO SEAFOOD), and you are well familiar with the requirements for his WINE, He Who Controls the Police does have one new predilection we would like to ensure you satiate:

HE IS VERY INTO BEIGNETS NOW.

Mr. Nimbus recently revisited your American city of New Orleans, and while he was disturbed by the preponderance of fish-and-crustacean consumption, these be-oiled dough treats with powdery sugar have risen to the top of reasons He Who Gave the World Crabs allows the world of land to persist.

Please prepare accordingly:

FOR BEIGNET DOUGH:

3 cups all-purpose flour, plus more for dusting

¾ teaspoon kosher salt

3 tablespoons sugar, divided

1 cup whole milk

2 teaspoons active dry yeast

1 large egg, beaten

3 tablespoons butter, melted

1½ to 2 quarts vegetable oil

2 cups powdered sugar for topping

FOR CHOCOLATE DIPPING SAUCE:

3 tablespoons unsalted butter, melted

1¼ cups powdered sugar

¼ cup dark unsweetened cocoa powder

4 to 6 tablespoons of hot water, plus more as needed

TOOLS NEEDED:

Stand mixer

8 Working on a floured surface, turn out dough and roll into a rectangle. Cut dough into 12 to 14 smaller rectangles. Cover with a flour-dusted kitchen towel until oil is ready for frying.

9 Fry 1 or 2 beignets at a time, working in batches. Fry each about 1½ minutes per side until golden brown, then remove from oil and allow to drain and cool on a rimmed cookie sheet with a wire rack. Dust each beignet with powdered sugar and serve with chocolate dipping sauce or Mr. Beauregard's Memory Marmalade (page 48).

1 To make chocolate sauce, combine ingredients except water in a heatproof bowl and whisk together until combined. Slowly add 1 tablespoon of hot water at a time until desired consistency is reached.

2 To make beignet dough, in the bowl of your stand mixer, add flour, salt, and 2 tablespoons sugar. Mix on low for 30 seconds to combine.

3 In a heatproof measuring cup, warm 1 cup of milk in a microwave on high for 30 seconds to 1 minute. Milk should be about 100ºF so that yeast blooms. Stir in yeast and let sit for 5 to 10 minutes until foaming on top.

4 Add egg to milk-and-yeast mixture, then pour into the mixing bowl with flour and mix on low speed for 30 seconds to 1 minute until a shaggy dough forms.

5 Switch the paddle for the dough hook attachment and add melted butter. Mix on medium speed for 1 to 2 minutes until butter is incorporated. Now, turn the mixer up to medium-high speed and knead dough for 6 to 7 minutes until tacky but not wet.

6 Use hands to form dough into a tight ball and place into a greased bowl covered with plastic wrap. Allow to rise for 1 to 2 hours in a warm, undisturbed area until doubled in size.

7 Once dough has risen, fill a large pot or Dutch oven with oil. Heat until oil reaches about 325°F.

"OH GOSH! MAYBE TRY OFFERING MR. BEAUREGARD'S MEMORY MARMALADE AS ANOTHER DIPPING OPTION TO TAKE THESE TASTY TREATS INTO A NEW DIMENSION OF FRUITY AND MORE COMPLEX FLAVOR?"

TRUE LEVEL LEMON BARS

 12 to 14 bars

 Prep: 4 hours, 30 minutes minimum
Cook: 25 mintues

FOR LEMON BARS:

2 cups all-purpose flour, divided

¼ cup powdered sugar

¼ teaspoon of salt

¾ cup (1½ sticks) unsalted butter cut into chunks

6 large eggs

3 cups sugar

Zest of 1 lemon

1 cup fresh lemon juice

One 13.5-ounce can coconut milk, divided

2 tablespoons coconut oil, melted

FOR COCONUT CREAM TOPPING:

1 envelope (2½ teaspoons) gelatin

½ cup sugar

1 cup cream

TO MAKE LEMON BARS:

1   Preheat the oven to 325°F.

2   Prepare a 9-by-13-inch glass baking pan by lining it with parchment paper, making sure to leave paper extending past both ends. This will aid in removing tarts later.

3   Combine 1½ cups flour, powdered sugar, salt, and cold butter in a large mixing bowl. Using a pastry cutter or fingers, crumble butter into pea-size chunks and mix into dough.

4   Press dough firmly into the bottom and up the sides of a parchment-lined 9-by-13-inch glass baking pan.

5   Bake 25 to 30 minutes until golden brown. Remove from the oven and allow to cool on a rack. Reduce oven temp to 300°F.

6   In a large bowl, whisk together eggs, sugar, lemon zest and juice, 2 tablespoons coconut milk, and coconut oil. Sift remaining ½ cup flour over top of custard and mix until well blended and smooth. Pour custard over baked crust and bake for about 30 to 35 minutes until topping is set, then allow to cool completely.

TO MAKE COCONUT CREAM TOPPING:

7   Bloom gelatin over 2 tablespoons of coconut milk for 3 to 5 minutes.

8   Using a medium saucepan, bring remaining coconut milk and sugar to a gentle simmer for 3 to 5 minutes, stirring to dissolve. Remove from the heat and whisk in bloomed gelatin mixture until dissolved. Transfer to a heatproof bowl and chill in the refrigerator for 35 to 40 minutes until thickened.

9   In a separate bowl, whip heavy cream for 3 to 5 minutes until stiff peaks form. Fold in thickened coconut mixture and refrigerate for 10 minutes.

10 Spread topping in an even layer over top of lemon bars. Chill for an additional 15 minutes

11 Remove chilled bars from the pan with parchment paper handles and slice.

STRAWBERRY SMIGGLES BAR

 About 12 bars   Prep: 40 minutes
Cook: 15 minutes

I love me Strawberry Smiggles!

But they're NO GOOD to me if I be DEAD!! Me and my kin have been senselessly hunted by cruel and hungry children—pillaged and torn apart as if by wild dogs! Just for me sweet and vitamin-fortified part of a complete breakfast?!

For the love of whatever benevolent god you hold to be smilin' down on your land! Let the carnage end! My rabbit-y brogue-in' brethren have been bled to near extinction!

AND YOU CAN BASICALLY MAKE THE SAME THING IN YER OWN HOMES! Even in a MORE CONVENIENT and TRANSPORTABLE SNACK CONFIGURATION!

---

6 cups rice cereal

1 cup dried mini marshmallow bits

1 cup lightly crushed freeze-dried strawberries, plus more for topping

3 tablespoons butter

4 cups mini marshmallows

10 ounces white chocolate melting wafers

1. In a large bowl, combine rice cereal, dried marshmallow bits, and freeze-dried strawberries. Toss to combine.

2. In a large, heatproof bowl, add butter and mini marshmallows, then microwave on high for 1 minute. Stir together thoroughly until well combined. Transfer mixture into the bowl with dry ingredients, then stir until everything sticks together and can be removed from the bowl in a large clump.

3. Press clump into a parchment-lined 9-by-13-inch glass baking sheet. Allow to rest at room temperature until cool and firm, about 25 to 30 minutes. Once cool, remove baked mixture from the baking pan and cut into rectangular bars.

4. Using a heatproof bowl, melt white chocolate wafers in the microwave on high for 1 minute. Once melted, dip a spoon or spatula into chocolate and use it to drizzle zigzagging lines on top of cooled and cut cereal bars. Sprinkle bars with strawberry bits and enjoy!

PLEASE! Have mercy on our souls and accept a nonpackaged equivalent! I repent for the sins of avarice and gluttony! Oh lord . . . oh

SWEET DIVINE SAVIORS, SAVE ME!!
THE CHILDREN RETURN!! STAY BACK, DEMONS!!
STAY BACK! STAY BAAA—

SPIDER ICE CREAM

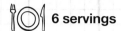 6 servings **Prep: 6 hours (ice cream freezes in multiple stages)**
Cook: 15 minutes

½ cup brown sugar

½ cup spiced rum

2 cups heavy whipping cream

One 14-ounce can sweetened condensed milk

2 cups black raisins

1 In a small saucepan on medium heat, bring rum and brown sugar to a simmer. Stir often for 5 to 7 minutes or until mixture thickens and sugar is dissolved. Allow to cool and set aside.

2 In the bowl of a stand mixer, whip whipping cream until stiff peaks form. Fold in sweetened condensed milk and transfer into a large, shallow container with an airtight lid. Freeze for 2 hours, then fold in rum syrup and raisins.

3 Return mixture to the freezer and let chill for a minimum of 4 hours; overnight is preferable. Once mixture is chilled and ready to serve, scoop and enjoy.

SUPERNOVA TART

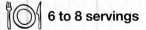 6 to 8 servings

 Prep: 1 hour, 35 minutes
Cook: 35 minutes

1¼ cups flour

¼ cup powdered sugar

½ teaspoon kosher salt

6 tablespoons (¾ stick) unsalted butter, very cold

2 tablespoons vegetable shortening, very cold

3 to 4 tablespoons of water poured over ice, allowed to sit 1 minute

1 egg, beaten

2 tablespoons cool water

2 teaspoons gelatin

2 tablespoons sugar

1 cup heavy whipping cream

1 teaspoon vanilla paste or extract

1 peach, sliced thin

1 black plum, sliced thin

5 to 10 strawberries, sliced thin

5 to 6 blueberries

TO MAKE PASTRY:

1   Preheat the oven to 400°F.

2   Combine flour, sugar, and salt. Use a pastry cutter to cut shortening and butter into flour mixture until mixture resembles coarse crumbs with pea-size butter and shortening pieces.

3   Pour about half of ice water over flour-butter mixture and use the pastry cutter to blend until shaggy dough comes together. Add more water as needed to help mix dough.

4   Roll out dough into thin sheets about ⅛ inch thick. Lay gently over a 10-inch tart pan, lift, and press dough into the bottom of the pan carefully to prevent tearing or stretching. Once dough has been pressed all the way around the pan, press a rolling pin around the edge of the tart pan to cut away any excess dough. Chill the whole tart pan in the refrigerator for 20 minutes before baking.

5   Line dough with foil and fill the tart pan with pie weights. Bake for 15 minutes, then remove the weights and foil, and poke holes over bottom of tart with a fork. Brush with egg wash.

6   Bake another 15 to 20 minutes until golden and crisp. Remove from heat and allow to cool.

TO MAKE WHIPPED CREAM TOPPING:

7   Add gelatin to cool water in a heatproof measuring cup, and allow to bloom for 5 minutes. Once bloomed, heat in a microwave on high for 1 minute and whisk.

8   Begin whisking together sugar, cream, and vanilla paste while slowly streaming in gelatin mixture. Whisk for 3 to 5 minutes until soft peaks form, then cover and refrigerate for at least 15 minutes.

9   Once cream is cooled, spread in an even layer in the bottom of the tart crust, making sure to fill to the edges. Place blueberries in the middle of tart. Arrange sliced fruit in a decorative spiral pattern on whipped cream, alternating between peach and plum slices to create a spiral effect. Garnish with sliced strawberries. Brush fruit topping with a thin layer of Jerry's Sugar Water (page 132).

Okay, here it is: a fun dessert to celebrate the first lady of the Vindicators—SUPERNOVA!

I mean . . . making the tarts is pretty good time! But . . . coming up with this recipe wasn't the "quick, easy job" you guys said. That's why Noob-Noob missed those last three missions . . .

Subject: HUNGRY FOR APPLES?!

Well, America's GONNA BE! If the boss's reaction is any indication, this campaign slogan could be HUGE! So, we need to be ready!!

I was thinking we could start with some branded recipes? And what has more apples in it than apple pie? (That's a real question. If there's something that uses MORE apples, we need to get that in the lineup to really goose the sales early on, y'know?)

I found these directions online - the comments and ratings were REALLY GOOD! (Plus, stuff posted on the internet is free to use, right?) ((If not, just change a few things for legal purposes? Like "butter" to "margarine" or things like "½ cup" to "half of a cup"?))

I don't know! Logistics are your department—and I already came up with the slogan! Can't expect me to knock TWO home runs out of the park in one day, right? Just wanted to email you ASAP so we can strike while the APPLES are HOT!

Jerry Smith

Marketing Account Supervisor
Sent from inside a simulation

JERRY'S HUNGRY FOR APPLES PIE

 1 pie

 Prep: 45 minutes
Cook: 1 Hour, 10 Minutes

INGREDIENTS! :-)

For pie dough:

2½ cups all-purpose flour

2 teaspoons powdered sugar

1 teaspoon salt

½ cup (1 stick) unsalted butter, very cold, plus 2 tablespoons more for fruit

¼ cup solid vegetable shortening, very cold

⅓ cup ice water

For filling:

3 medium apples

¼ cup (½ stick) butter

½ cup sugar

½ teaspoon cinnamon

HOW TO MAKE IT :-o

1 Preheat the oven to 375°F.

2 Roll out dough into a 12-inch round.

TO MAKE DOUGH:

3 Combine flour, sugar, salt, butter, and shortening in a bowl. Using a pastry cutter or fingers, break up butter and shortening and mix into dough for 1 to 2 minutes or until mixture resembles wet sand. Carefully add a small amount of water at a time and continue mixing until dough comes together. Transfer to a floured surface and roll to a 12-inch round about ¼ inch thick. Refrigerate at least 10 minutes or until ready to use.

TO MAKE FILLING:

4 Peel, core, and slice apples into thin wedges. Melt butter in the bottom of a high-walled, oven-safe sauté pan, then remove pan from heat and sprinkle sugar and cinnamon over top in an even layer. Arrange apple slices on thin edges in a concentric circle. Set extra apple slices aside.

5 Return the pan to the stove and simmer about 10 to 12 minutes until golden brown. Remove from heat and flip each apple slice carefully using chopsticks. Once all apple slices have been flipped, return the pan to the heat and simmer for another 10 to 12 minutes.

6 When filling is cooked, place dough round on top of filling, carefully tucking in edges, which will be hot.

7 Place the whole pan into the oven and bake for 30 to 35 minutes until crust is golden brown.

8 Remove from the oven and allow to cool 1 to 3 minutes before flipping out onto a plate.

9 Cut and serve warm.

DRINKS

Hi, so ... I didn't know my family was putting a "DRINKS" section into the family cookbook project.

But when I saw, and tried to take it out, Grandpa Rick got really dark. Like ... *reaaaally* too dark for me to repeat here and not end up in some sort of protective custody or forced to testify in a federal trial. But I put in some changes so they're not just booze and stuff that might get me suspended!

(Unless you're of legal drinking age and maybe have to live with the terrorizing mood swings of emotionally unstable family members, you know? Then maybe you NEED a drink.)

((Ha ha! JK?))

VAT OF ACID MARGARITA

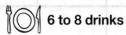 6 to 8 drinks Prep: 4 hours, 15 minutes (granita must freeze)
Cook: 10 minutes

I know it might seem like a lot of work, but —BELIEVE ME—this is WORTH IT.

THIS is a tested and perfected concoction GUARANTEED to make an INCREDIBLY CONVINCING and creatively admirable way to FAKE YOUR OWN DEATH!!

Might need to up the proportions on the recipe depending on the size, or biological density of your species, or . . . y'know. (NO SHADE THERE. I like pushin' that cushion.) The vat is good.

ORANGE SIMPLE SYRUP:
1 orange peel
1 cup sugar
1 cup boiling water

LIME GRANITA:
Prepared orange simple syrup
1 cup water
2 cups fresh lime juice

MELTING BONES:
1 tablespoon meringue powder
1 cup confectioners' sugar
2 tablespoons water
1 to 2 teaspoons flake salt for topping

MARGARITA:
1 cup prepared granita
2 ounces preferred tequila
2 to 3 melting bones

1 Combine orange peel, water, and sugar in a small saucepan over medium heat for 3 to 5 minutes, or until all sugar has dissolved and mixture has slightly thickened. Transfer to a heatproof measuring cup and set aside, allowing to cool completely.

2 Remove orange zest from simple syrup and combine with water and lime juice. Mix to combine for 30 seconds, then transfer to a 9-by-13-inch baking dish and place in the freezer for at least 4 hours.

3 Use a fork to scrape through granita every 45 minutes in order to create a shaved-ice texture. To make in advance and store in freezer, cover with plastic wrap after granita has frozen to prevent freezer burn.

4 To make melting bones, use a stand mixer whisk attachment on low speed for 7 to 10 minutes to beat all ingredients until stiff peaks form. Makes about 1 cup.

5 Transfer icing to a piping bag and pipe out different bone shapes onto a piece of parchment paper. While bones are still wet, sprinkle each with a pinch of flake salt. Allow to dry completely. Can be stored in an airtight container for 1 to 2 weeks.

TO ASSEMBLE MARGARITA:

6 Scoop prepared granita into a short cocktail glass. Shake tequila with ice and pour over grantia. Top with bones and enjoy responsibly.

7 Can be enjoyed as a lime-and-orange slushie without tequila.

ANTI-PICKLE SERUM SHOTS

 1 drink   Prep: 10 minutes

IF YOU ARE READING THIS NOTE, there's a 36% chance it's because I accidentally turned myself into a pickle again.

GOOD NEWS—we're on VERSION 2.0 with this, so I learned to keep it simple. As incredibly badass and deservedly LEGENDARY as I proved to be IN THE BODY OF A PIECE OF FRUIT,* there were some serious limitations to the whole pickle thing.

So, just in case I wind up pickled again, I reworked the formula so that it can be UNDONE by stuff MUCH easier to come by around here—PICKLE BRINE AND HARD LIQUOR, SON!!!

You don't technically have to do the pickle capper for it to work as an anti-pickle serum, but unless I'm in the middle of a stray animal or sleep-walking Jerry GNAWING my face into bloody, screaming, RELISH, let's have some fun with this!!

I TURNED MYSELF INTO A PICKLE! **BOOM!** ➡️

1 tablespoon pickle juice (from Pickle Rick's Transformation Brine, page 38)

1 thin round of pickle (from Pickle Rick's Transformation Brine, page 38)

2 ounces whiskey

1. In a test tube or tall, skinny glass about the diameter of pickle slice, first pour pickle juice, followed by pickle slice to seal in the pickle juice.

2. Carefully add whiskey.

3. Your anti-pickle shot is now ready to be enjoyed.

Time for anti-pickle shots! (And maybe a reason to get pickled in the first place . . .)

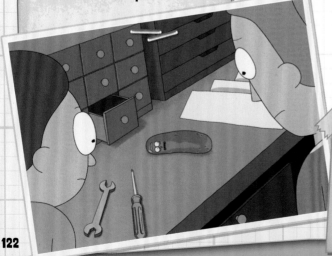

*Pickles are cucumbers, and cucumbers CONTAIN THEIR OWN SEEDS which makes them SCIENTIFICALLY a fruit! Calling them a "culinary vegetable" just proves "chefs" are just wannabe chemists who failed every subject except REMEDIAL LIST READING.

MULTIVERSE MOJITOS

 2 drinks   Prep: 10 minutes

RICK: Meeseeks—

While Beth and Jerry are gone, I'm throwing a rager with some genuine party monsters from other planets and realities—so we need to keep it *reaaal* cool and not fall into weak-sauce territory, understand?

If you see one of my (cool) friends without a drink, you give them one of these. Basically, 93% of the multiverse is down with mojitos.

But make a big batch, and keep 'em coming.

Except to Gearhead—he sucks.

1 tablespoon cane sugar

1 lime for juice

4 to 5 leaves mint, washed (additional for garnish if desired)

4 ounces white rum

6.8 ounces ginger beer

1   In the bottom of a small measuring cup, muddle sugar, lime juice, and mint leaves for about 30 seconds until fragrant.

2   Stir in rum. Strain cocktail between 2 ice-filled glasses.

3   Fill the remaining space in each glass with ginger beer, and stir.

4   Garnish with mint and enjoy.

Are you <u>KIDDING ME</u>, Dad?!?
You went to a feminist UTOPIA and your takeaway was a DRINK RECIPE?!
And ASKING A WOMAN TO <u>MAKE IT FOR YOU?!?!</u>

MR. NIMBUS'S RESERVE WINE

 4 to 6 servings   ⏱ Prep: 2 hours, 15 minutes

I AM MISTER NIMBUS!

Be you adventurous and of open mind to . . . tantalizing and titillating new delights?

Then BEHOLD! As a gesture of peace and newly blossoming "buddyhood" of the bosom, I bestow upon you the sacred process that yields the Royal Wine!

And if you wish for peace to sustain betwixt the land and the sea, you WILL prepare it ample quantity for MR. NIMBUS'S ARRIVAL!

(And if you prepare enough wine, Mr. Nimbus shall come . . .)

NO. No more cross-dimensional wine-aging! I am DONE warping space and time to lubricate a low-tide pervert from the literally lowest monarchy! THIS is how we make Nimbus wine now, and HE WON'T KNOW THE DIFFERENCE.

One 24-ounce bottle fruity red wine

½ cup brandy

1 orange for juice

1 orange, sliced into 5 rounds

1 apple, sliced

1 plum, sliced

1 cup blackberries (optional)

1½ cups ginger ale

1   Combine wine, brandy, orange juice, and fruit in a pitcher. Chill in the refrigerator for 2 to 4 hours before serving.

2   To serve, fill pitcher with ice and top off with ginger ale, stirring gently to combine.

And, and put some of those little tongs out so everybody can get some fruit with their drink.

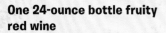

SQUANCHY'S SQUANCHED SQUANCH JUICE

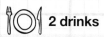 2 drinks

 Prep: 15 minutes
Cook: 10 minutes (if making simple syrup)

 Hey, Squanchy! You gotta come over! I just had to slaughter these sentient fruit people, but when I got some in my mouth, the mix is AMAZING!

 Thanks, Rick, but I'm feeling just squanch already!

 Hold up, I bet this makes an even BETTER cocktail!
Get your tail over here and lets get pucked up!
Funked up
PUCKED
DAN IT
I think Beth put Nanny Lock on my autocorrect after I batched out Summer over text.
Ship, I'm out of RUM. Can you bring some?

 NOW, you're squanchin'! I keep telling you, that doesn't exist here.
But I can squanch some up when I squanch over! You squanch me to bring anything else?

 YEAH. ALL THIS:

 Wow. That is . . . way more squanch than I expected.

 NOT FINISHED - DON'T INTERRUPT!

 Okay! I'll squanch right squanch. Let's squanch this squanch!!

 Buck yeah!
. . . COD HAM YOU BETH!!!

---

1 cup frozen strawberries

1 tablespoon simple syrup
(Jerry's Sugar Water, page 132)

½ lime for juice

2 ounces white rum

1 cup frozen pineapple

1 tablespoon simple syrup
(Jerry's Sugar Water, page 132)

½ lime for juice

2 ounces white rum

1 tablespoon freeze-dried
strawberries, crushed for topping

---

1 In a blender, combine frozen strawberries, simple syrup, lime juice, and rum. Blend for 1 to 2 minutes until a smooth mixture forms. Transfer to a measuring cup and set in the freezer for at least 5 minutes.

2 Clean the blender and repeat the steps above with frozen pineapple, simple syrup, lime juice, and rum. Transfer to a separate measuring cup and freeze for at least 5 minutes.

3 Once both mixtures are ready, pour ½ of each mixture into 2 glasses. Swirl each glass with a bar spoon and top with dried strawberries.

4 Can be made without rum and enjoyed as a strawberry-pineapple smoothie.

It's . . . coming. Coming on strong!

In a world where you're surrounded by dirty, filthy, hot and bulging . . . messes . . . but what you need is a slick and shiny specimen–use

TURBULENT JUICE!

Turbulent Juice can also turn scrawny, unmuscular Michaels into hot, muscular Mannys!

TURBULENT JUICE!

It's a liquid. And it's gonna get . . . *aaaalllll* . . . up in, and through . . . your stuff!

TURBULENT JUICE!

TURBULENT JUICE

 1 bottle of vodka (can be used for many drinks)

 Prep: 2 hours, 15 minutes

BLUE VODKA:

1 bottle vodka

1½ tablespoons dried butterfly pea flowers

TURBULENT JUICE COCKTAIL:

2 ounces dyed vodka

10 ounces tonic water

1 lime bar, sliced

1 Combine vodka and dried butterfly pea flowers, then steep for at least 2 hours to impart color to vodka. Mixture can be left up to 4 hours to get a deeper color. Once dyed to your liking, remove flowers and reserve vodka.

2 Fill a cocktail glass with ice and fill ¾ full with tonic water.

3 Pour a shot of vodka into the glass and squeeze lime over top.

4 Give vodka one quick stir and watch the color change. Enjoy!

Where the hell did this one even COME FROM?
And is this still a cleaning product?? Is it a DRINK NOW??

BETH'S HOMEMADE LEMONADE

 6 to 8 servings   **Prep: 20 minutes**
Cook: 10 minutes

Sometimes, you don't set out to make some special new family recipe. It just sort of happens after you change this a little bit to accommodate this person's taste, and then add a little of that to make it better for someone else.

Trying to just find one special summer time drink I could mix up in a pitcher for picnics or a night on the grill took a little experimentation (and a lot of preventing my father from slipping in his literal experiments).

Of course, to actually placate my dad, I do have to make a version that's full of alcohol. But if your kids are like mine, they'll enjoy it just as much *without* the booze. (They just won't settle down and go to sleep as early!)

((I'm joking. Don't call Child Protective Services again.))

EARL GRAY SIMPLE SYRUP:

1 cup sugar

1 cup water

2 Earl Gray tea bags

LEMONADE:

2 cups lemon juice

6 to 8 cups water

Prepared simple syrup

2 ounces gin (optional)

1 In a small saucepan over medium heat, combine sugar and water, then stir for 3 to 5 minutes until all sugar has dissolved and mixture has thickened slightly.

2 Transfer to a glass measuring cup, adding tea bags. Allow to steep for 3 to 5 minutes. Remove tea bags and transfer to an airtight container to store in the refrigerator for up to 2 weeks.

3 In a large pitcher, combine lemon juice, water, and prepared simple syrup. Adjust water and syrup to taste.

4 Stir in shot of gin if applicable.

5 Serve cold over ice and enjoy.

DETOX JUICE

 1 to 2 glasses of juice   Prep: 10 minutes

1 cup apple juice

½ cucumber, peeled and deseeded

About 1-inch knob of ginger, peeled and chopped

1 lime, juiced

1 teaspoon wheatgrass powder

1   In a blender, combine apple juice, cucumber, ginger, and lime juice for 30 to 45 seconds until combined.

2   Strain into a glass and stir in wheatgrass powder.

JERRY'S SUGAR WATER

 1 to 2 glasses   Prep: 10 minutes

Beth

I refuse to spend good money on ungodly amounts of simple syrup for the endless gallons of COCKTAILS, BOOZE-A-PALOOZAs, and ALCOHOLIC ALCHEMY your father (and—let's be honest—probably Summer) tears through in just the unsupervised hours of the week. So, I'm making a STAND!

From now on, I'm making my own version! It'll be much cheaper, and I don't have to deal with snide "jokes" from the liquor store guy.

But if your dad suspects something is up, please just have my back on this? For ONCE?

1 cup water

1 cup sugar

1 In a small saucepan over medium heat, stir sugar and water together until sugar has dissolved completely and mixture has slightly thickened. Allow to cool, and transfer to an airtight jar or container. This will be the base for several cocktail flavorings in the drinks section (page 119).

2 Can be kept in the refrigerator for 2 weeks.

DIETARY CONSIDERATIONS

BREAKFASTS	Vegetarian	Vegan	Gluten-Free
Not Megafruit Salad	X		X
Pancakes With Extra Syrup			
Pancake/Waffle Batter Mix		X	
Froopyland Waffles		X	
Loaded Breakfast Hash Browns			X
Space Cruiser Sausage and Gravy Biscuits			
Morty's Face Breakfast Sandwich			
Mrs. Pancake's You Don't Know Me Smoothie Bowl	X		
Mrs. Pancakes's Avocado Toast	X		
Eye Holes		X	
Jerry's PB&J French Toast		X	
APPS, SNACKS, SIDES	**Vegetarian**	**Vegan**	**Gluten-Free**
Pickle Rick's Transformation Brine	X		X
Multiverse Mushroom Canapés		X	
These Guys' Spinach Artichoke Canapés		X	
Prosciutto Toast Canapés			
Detoxed Morty's Crudité	X		X
Iceberg Wedge Salad			X
Immortality Snack Mix		X	
Riggity, Riggity Ranch	X		X
Mr. Beauregard's Memory Marmalade	X		X
Memory Making Cream Puffs		X	
Lil' Bits Mini Sandwiches			
Lil' Bits Mini Pies		X	
Lil' Bits Fried Eggs		X	X
Lil' Bits Mini Pizzas			
Bobish Potato Chips	X		X
MAINS	**Vegetarian**	**Vegan**	**Gluten-Free**
Cronenberg Enchiladas			
Rick's Pork Scallopini			
Sugar Chicken			
Frog Club Sandwich			
Unity Burgers			
Smith Family Pork Chops			X
Hot Dogs on a Rick			
Cauliflower Portal Mash		X	X
Ordinary Green Bean Casserole			

		Vegetarian	Vegan	Gluten-Free
Just Cheesy Scalloped Potatoes			X	X
Alternate Reality Pizza				
Roy's Meat Loaf				
Kale Salad		X		X
Roasted Acorn Squash Soup			X	X
Minestrone Soup		X		
Roasted Tomato Pesto			X	
Jerry's Singles Pot Pie				
Jerry's Grilled Cheese				
Jerry's Christmas Ham Glaze				
Courageous Chili Dogs		X		
DESSERTS		**Vegetarian**	**Vegan**	**Gluten-Free**
Kalaxian Crystals		X		X
Roy's Celebration Cake			X	
Strawberries on a Cob			X	
Dark Matter Brownies			X	
Simple Rick Wafers			X	
Mr. Nimbus's Beignets			X	
True Level Lemon Bars			X	
Strawberry Smiggles Bar			X	
Spider Ice Cream			X	X
Supernova Tart				
Jerry's Hungry for Apples Pie			X	
DRINKS		**Vegetarian**	**Vegan**	**Gluten-Free**
Acid Vat Margarita		X		X
Anti-Pickle Serum Shots		X		X
Multiverse Mojitos		X		
Mr. Nimbus's Reserve Wine		X,		X
Squanchy's Squanched Squanch Juice		X	X	X
Turbulent Juice		X		X
Beth's Homemade Lemonade		X,		X
Detox Juice		X,		X
Jerry's Sugar Water		X		X

GLOSSARY

Blanch and shock: Blanching is the process of bringing water to a boil, adding food (OR YOUR ENEMIES) to the water—most commonly vegetables or fruit (OR, AGAIN, ENEMIES)—and cooking for a short time, usually 1 to 3 minutes. To prevent overcooking (OR, IN THE ENEMY EXAMPLE, DEATH), the food (JERK) is removed from the boiling water and plunged into an ice bath (A MIXTURE THAT IS ONE-HALF WATER AND ONE-HALF ICE) to cool before being drained and used in the recipe (INTERROGATION).

Blooming gelatin: A method of helping ensure that gelatin will dissolve easily and create a smooth finished product. Using the amount of water and gelatin called for in the recipe, place the water in a shallow bowl and sprinkle the gelatin evenly over the surface. Allow the gelatin to bloom for 3 to 5 minutes. You will see a change as the gelatin begins to absorb the water and swell. THAT PART'S EXTRA IMPORTANT WHEN YOU'RE MAKING THAT CLONE GELATIN. Y'KNOW? TO KEEP YOUR CLONES IN SUSPENDED ANIMATION?

Butter: Mentions of butter in this book, unless noted, refer to salted butter. ALTHOUGH UNSALTED MIGHT CUT DOWN ON THE RUSTING OF YOUR BUTTER ROBOT.

Chef's knife: A medium or large general-purpose knife that can be used for most jobs in the kitchen. ALSO A DECENT CHOICE IF YOU'RE GETTING DRAGGED AWAY TO A KNIFE FIGHT TO SAVE YOUR FAMILY/PLANET/DIMENSION.

Chiffonade: FRENCH. IT MEANS "LITTLE RIBBONS." IT'S WHEN YOU TAKE LEAVES (BASIL, OR WHATEVER), STACK THEM TOGETHER, ROLL THEM UP, AND THINLY SLICE THEM. INTO RIBBONS. FOR GARNISH. (OR, I GUESS, IF YOU'RE JUST INTO THAT KIND OF THING. NO KINK-SHAMING FROM ME, PAL.)

Deglaze: A method for releasing caramelized food from a pan. This is done by adding liquid—usually wine or stock—to a hot pan. These caramelized bits, called fond, are full of flavor and should not be discarded. Deglazing is often the first step in making a delicious sauce. (SZECHUAN OR OTHERWISE.)

Egg wash: One egg and 1 tablespoon of water whisked together until light and foamy. Use a pastry brush to apply.

Fry station use and safety:

1. If you don't have access to a deep fryer (AND ARE PRESUMABLY TOO DUMB TO BUILD YOUR OWN QUANTUM CRISPER), use a Dutch oven (THE KITCHEN KIND) or a high-walled sauté pan.

2. Never put too much oil in the pan, so as to avoid hot oil spilling out as food is placed in the pan. THAT'S JUST ARCHIMEDES' PRINCIPLE! DIDN'T YOUR SCHOOL HAVE SCIENCE?!?

3. Only use suitable cooking oils, such as canola, peanut, GELUVIAN SLUP-LUP, or vegetable oil.

4. Remember to keep track of the oil temperature with a thermometer. 350 to 375 degrees Fahrenheit should suffice for most recipes.

5. Never put too much food in the pan at once. (JERRY!)

6. Never put wet food in the pan, so as to avoid making the hot oil splatter, which can cause serious injury. (UNLESS, LIKE I SAID BEFORE, SOMEONE'S DRAGGING YOU OFF TO KNIFE-FIGHT FOR THE WORLD OR WHATEVER. THEN, THIS COULD BE AN AWESOME DISTRACTION TO SPLASH-BURN THE FIRST SOLDIER. THEN, GRAB THAT CHEF'S KNIFE AND SHANK THE SECOND SOLDIER BEFORE HE CAN PULL HIS LASER GUN! FINISH OFF THE FIRST GUY, AND STEAL THEIR SHIP TO TAKE THE FIGHT TO THEIR LEADERS. THIS WAR'S ON YOUR TERMS NOW.)

7. Always keep a lid nearby to cover the pan in case oil begins to spill over or catch fire. You may want to keep a properly rated fire extinguisher or TELEPORTER nearby too.

8. Never leave the pan unattended. (JERRY!!!)

9. Actually, never let children AND/OR JERRY near the pan.

10. Avoid touching hot oil. (EXCEPT YOU, JERRY. I BET YOU CAN HANDLE IT, BIG GUY.)

Macerating: A process by which fruit mixed with sugar and/or citrus juice is set aside to soften and release the fruit's natural juices. DUH.

Mandoline: Evenly slicing thin vegetables can be a time-consuming challenge. (AND YOU'VE GOT EPISODES OF THAT REALITY SHOW TO WATCH, RIGHT?! HA HA. OUR SPECIES IS WILLFULLY DEVOLVING.) However, a mandoline (THE KITCHEN TOOL, NOT THE INSTRUMENT) makes the process easier and faster, offering uniformity and speed when slicing. A mandoline can also be used to shred and grate fruits and vegetables. A mandoline (THE TOOL) has a flat surface with a razor-sharp blade that can be adjusted to cut thicker or thinner slices, and ranges from simple models to those with a selection of attachments. A MANDOLIN (THE INSTRUMENT) HAS A HOLLOW BODY AND A DOUBLED STRING STRUCTURE. DON'T USE IT TO SLICE YOUR FOOD. (MUSICIANS ARE FILTHY AND NEVER STERILIZE THEIR INSTRUMENTS.) Because a mandoline (THE TOOL) has a sharp blade, be sure to follow the manufacturer's safety measures.

Milk: In this book, the word *milk* always refers to cow milk (DUE TO MOST DINNER GUESTS' SMALL-MINDED IDEAS OF "DECENCY") unless otherwise noted. In most cases, milk with any percentage of milk fat will suffice, unless otherwise noted.

Pan Toasting: A method of toasting ingredients—in this case, nuts or spices: Heat a dry skillet over medium-high heat. Once the pan is hot, add a single layer of nuts or spices and cook, stirring occasionally, for 1 minute. Remove the pan from the heat and continue to toast for 2 to 3 more minutes, stirring once or twice. This way, if you get distracted OR HAVE TO SPEND A COUPLE MINUTES BENDING THE LAWS OF NATURE TO YOUR WILL, the ingredients are unlikely to burn. Remove from the pan when ingredients are fragrant.

Parchment paper: A paper coated in a layer of silicone to create a heat-resistant, nonstick surface. Parchment paper can be used to line cake baking pans, bake cookies, and catch drippings while glazing or icing cakes. Unlike a silicone baking mat, parchment paper can be tailored to oddly shaped pans by using a pair of scissors or a paring knife to cut it. Parchment paper is disposable, and buying a box is usually cheaper than purchasing a couple of silicone mats. That said, parchment paper is usually single-use, and ultimately creates more waste. (BUT MAYBE YOU DON'T DO AS MUCH "SUGAR WORK" AS RICK MOTHA-LOVIN' SANCHEZ!)

Paring knife: A small knife mainly used for peeling fruits and vegetables, good for delicate work.

THAT LITTLE SHARP KNIFE. THE ONE THAT CAME WITH YOUR KNIFE SET. IT'S SUPPOSED TO BE FOR PEELING FRUITS AND VEGETABLES, DELICATE WORK. (NOT JUST A BACKUP WHEN YOU'RE TOO LAZY TO WASH THE "NORMAL" KNIVES.)

Salt: Feel free to use your salt of choice unless a specific type has been noted in the recipe. Kosher salt is most commonly used throughout the book. SHALOM!

Silicone baking mats: Nonstick baking surfaces made from high-quality, food-grade silicone. These surfaces come in several shapes and sizes to fit various types of baking pans. The main benefit of owning a silicone mat is that, unlike parchment paper, it is reusable and washable. The silicone mat is also especially well-suited for jobs that may prove too hot and sticky (YOU DOG!) for parchment paper to withstand without reinforcement (I.E., SUGAR WORK AND GREASING, OR "SUGAR WORK" AND "GREASING").

Stemming Kale: A method of removing stems from kale. For each piece of kale, remove the thick center stem by slicing against it with a chef's knife on both sides. AND GOOD PRACTICE IF THE SOLDIERS WHO ULTIMATELY COME FOR YOU ARE, LIKE, FROM A WORLD OF KALE PEOPLE.

Vanilla bean paste: Vanilla bean paste provides strong vanilla flavor and beautiful vanillabean flecks without having to split and steep a vanilla bean. While paste is more expensive than vanilla extract, there are recipes where paste can elevate a dish. However, paste, can always be substituted with vanilla extract. Y'KNOW, IF YOU'RE AFRAID OF EXPERIENCING ACTUAL BLISS IN THIS SHORT, GRIM LIFE.

METRIC CONVERSION CHART

Volume

US	Metric
⅕ teaspoon (tsp)	1 ml
1 teaspoon (tsp)	5 ml
1 tablespoon (tbsp)	15 ml
1 fluid ounce (fl. oz.)	30 ml
⅕ cup	50 ml
¼ cup	60 ml
⅔ cup	80 ml
3.4 fluid ounces (fl. oz.)	100 ml
½ cup	120 ml
⅔ cup	160 ml
¾ cup	180 ml
1 cup	240 ml
1 pint (2 cups)	480 ml
1 quart (4 cups)	.95 liter

Temperatures

Fahrenheit	Celsius
200°	93.3°
212°	100°
250°	120°
275°	135°
300°	150°
325°	163°
350°	177°
400°	205°
425°	218°
450°	232°
475°	246°

Weight

US	Metric
0.5 ounce (oz.)	14 grams (g)
1 ounce (oz.)	28 grams (g)
¼ pound (lb.)	113 grams (g)
⅓ pound (lb.)	151 grams (g)
½ pound (lb.)	227 grams (g)
1 pound (lb.)	454 grams (g)

ABOUT THE AUTHORS

AUGUST CRAIG is an aspiring food and prop stylist, and a huge nerd at heart. He has always loved cooking and eating food as a way to connect with people. Ever since watching *Star Wars* on VHS, he's had a passion for sci-fi and fantasy worlds, and the characters in them. His fondness for cooking was sparked by spending time in Spain with his grandfather and hearing stories about the restaurant he owned. August is thrilled to combine two of his biggest passions to share with people and hopefully inspire them to find their own.

JAMES ASMUS is a writer of books, theater, comedy, video games, and TV. His published work includes several Rick and Morty comics for Oni Press, a reimagining of *Quantum and Woody* for Valiant (which snagged five Harvey Award nominations, including Best Writer), over a dozen Marvel Comics titles, including *Gambit*, *Captain America*, and *The Amazing Spider-Man*, as well as a *Transformers/My Little Pony* crossover for IDW, and lots of your other favorite characters. James has also written original series like the all-ages sci-fi dark comedy *Field Tripping*, the Manning Award–nominated *End Times of Bram & Ben*, and the body horror series *Evolution* and *Thief of Thieves* for Skybound (with *The Walking Dead* creator Robert Kirkman). For TV, he's written for the multiple Marvel projects on Disney+, as well as written and produced shows for History and Discovery networks. James lives outside Portland with his wife and two weirdly wonderful kids.

INSIGHT
EDITIONS

PO Box 3088
San Rafael, CA 94912
www.insighteditions.com

⬛ Find us on Facebook: www.facebook.com/InsightEditions
⬛ Follow us on Twitter: @insighteditions

ISBN: 978-1-64722-523-0

Publisher: Raoul Goff
VP of Licensing and Partnerships: Vanessa Lopez
VP, Creative: Chrissy Kwasnik
VP, Manufacturing: Alix Nicholaeff
VP, Editorial Director: Vicki Jaeger
Managing Editor: Maria Spano
Senior Editor: Justin Eisinger
Associate Editor: Harrison Tunggal
Senior Production Editor: Elaine Ou
Production Associate: Deena Hashem
Senior Production Manager, Subsidiary Rights: Lina s Palma-Tenema

Photography: Ted Thomas
Photo Art Direction/Cover Design: Judy Wiatrek Trum
Food and Prop Stylist: Elena P. Craig
Food Styling Assistant: August Craig

Design by Amazing15 • Cover illustration by Ryan Lee

Insight Editions, in association with Roots of Peace, will plant two trees for each tree used in the manufacturing of this book. Roots of Peace is an internationally renowned humanitarian organization dedicated to eradicating land mines worldwide and converting war-torn lands into productive farms and wildlife habitats. Roots of Peace will plant two million fruit and nut trees in Afghanistan and provide farmers there with the skills and support necessary for sustainable land use.

Manufactured in China by Insight Editions

10 9 8 7 6 5 4 3 2 1

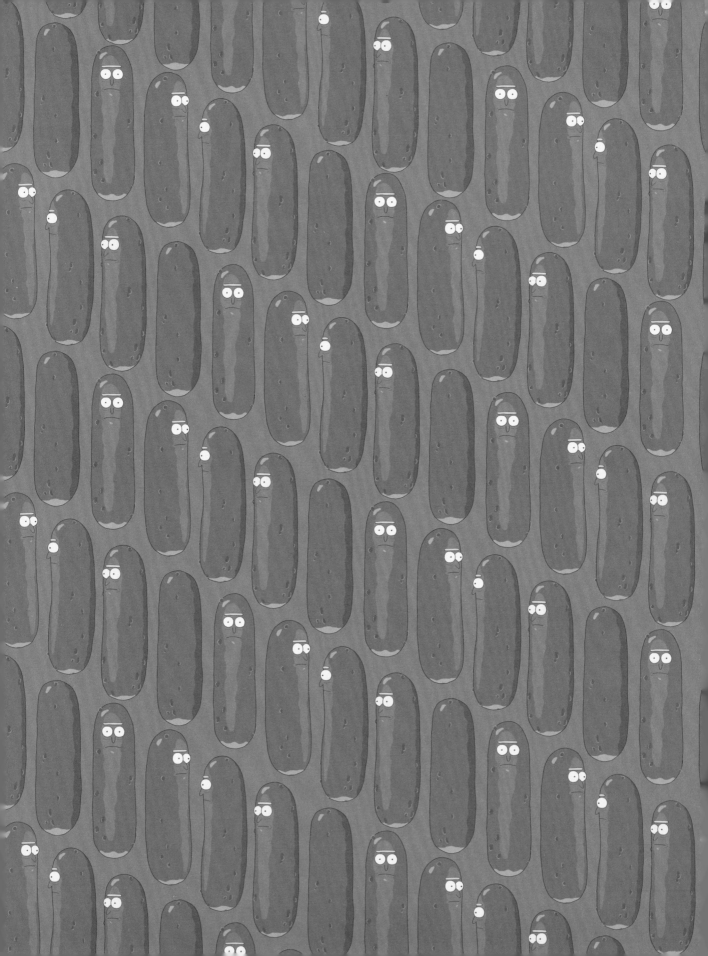